Cultural Revolution

A Captivating Guide to the Cultural Revolution and Mao Zedong

Free Bonus from Captivating History (Available for a Limited time)

Hi History Lovers!

Now you have a chance to join our exclusive history list so you can get your first history ebook for free as well as discounts and a potential to get more history books for free! Simply visit the link below to join.

Captivatinghistory.com/ebook

Also, make sure to follow us on Facebook, Twitter and Youtube by searching for Captivating History.

Contents

Part 1: The Cultural Revolution

A Captivating Guide to a Decade-Long Upheaval in China Unleashed by Mao Zedong to Preserve Chinese Communism

Introduction

The Cultural Revolution, formally known as the "Great Proletarian Cultural Revolution," was begun by Mao Zedong, the chairman of the Communist Party of China, as a means of quashing capitalism in China. He wanted to ensure that the desire for a communist government would remain strong in the country long after his death. Like other previous leaders who attempted to continue to rule after their death, his attempt did not work out quite the way he had planned.

Over the course of a decade, from the summer of 1966 to 1976, Mao Zedong implemented a number of changes that have led him to be known as one of the most brutal tyrants of the modern age. It is estimated that between 500,000 to two million Chinese people, although numbers can go as high as twenty million, died as a direct result of Zedong's Cultural Revolution. It also resulted in millions of people being imprisoned, displaced, and tortured in an attempt to cement Mao Zedong's reputation as the leader of the communist world.

By 1966, the enthusiasm for the new form of government that had helped Mao Zedong rise to power had begun to wane. People had become disillusioned, as the economy was in bad shape and the promises that had been made had not come to fruition. Much like communism in Russia under Joseph Stalin, only a few people at the top had actually benefited from the changes.

Mao Zedong had hoped to recapture the enthusiasm that had been lost and to consolidate his own power as the head of the Communist Party of China (CPC). Accusing an unseen group of capitalists as being the problem within the nation, he began to persecute anyone who he believed held capitalist ideals or anyone who stood against him. This included people within his own party who were attempting to help the economy recover. The declaration for the Cultural Revolution was made on May 16th, 1966, and it formally began in August of the same year.

Chapter 1 –Mao Zedong's Early Life, Rise to Power, and the Government Upheaval That Changed China during the First Half of the 20th Century

Mao Zedong is often named with some of the most notorious tyrants in modern history, including Adolf Hitler, Joseph Stalin, and Pol Pot. Like those despotic leaders, one of the most infamous Chinese leaders came from humble beginnings as well. In addition, Mao Zedong's rise to power followed a similar trajectory as theirs. As the people in China began to look at communism as a better system of government that would forward equality over the existing government, Mao joined the Revolution of 1911.

Just as Hitler, Stalin, and Pol Pot warped the trajectory of the revolutions in their own country to their benefit, Mao Zedong used the unrest to claim power for himself. And once he obtained that power, he refused to let it go. During the last decade of his life, Mao Zedong attempted to build his legacy, cementing it in a way that would permanently change China, but it would not end in the way that he had intended.

Early Life

Born on December 26th, 1893, Mao Zedong was raised in the small southeastern Chinese province of Hunan. He was the fourth child and the youngest son. Although his parents were considered peasants, his father owned several acres, usually estimated at about four acres. This was more than the majority of the other peasants in the area owned, making his family more distinguished than many of the peasants around them. Most of Mao's early years were spent helping around his parents' farm once he was old enough to take on easy tasks.

Despite their higher status based on their large property, they were not immune to the problems that arose in agrarian regions. In 1910, a famine plagued Hunan. During this time, Mao Zedong and his family would have felt the same poverty and pains as the other peasants around them.

When he was old enough to go to school, his father's position made it possible for the young boy to start getting an education. Over time, Mao Zedong because more interested in education than in helping his family, and this eventually led to a rift between him and his father. His education was only meant to help him better manage the accounts on the farm, not to instill ideas of politics. When Mao was thirteen years old, he was removed from primary school to work full-time on the farm. He was also forced to participate in an arranged marriage, one that he never consummated and never acknowledged. Since he never recognized her as his wife, Mao never lived with Luo Yixiu, and she died two years after their marriage.

In an act of rebellion against the familial expectations of him, Mao left home and moved to Changsha, the capital of the province of Hunan, around 1910.

Map of Hunan

(*Source: https://d-maps.com/m/asia/china/hunan/hunan25.gif*)

The Revolution of 1911 and Political Activism

The social unrest in China had begun some time before the 20th century began, with many of the people in power and intellectuals pushing for the country to strike out and create an empire as so many other nations had done. Others looked at the changes in the world and wanted to see China begin to become more modern so that it could keep up with technology and power structures. Ultimately, the intellectuals and people who wanted an empire would lose to those who wanted to improve China.

Map of China near the Turn of the Century

(*Source:*
https://en.wikipedia.org/wiki/File:1899_United_States_Government_Commercial_map_of_China,_showing_treaty_ports,_ports_of_foreign_control,_railways,_telegraphs,_waterways.jpg)

By 1910, the pressure for change passed a breaking point, as the Western world constantly pushed up against the East. Centuries of Western imperialism had changed the world, and by this point, it was affecting even the more powerful nations like China and Japan. With so much Western influence near their borders, the Chinese people in power wanted to strengthen their own country's position in the world.

However, the Qing Dynasty, which had been in control of China since 1636, had already proved that it was not interested in changing things as drastically as the people were demanding. This led to the formation of an anti-Qing activist group that was headed by Sun Yat-sen, who, among others, began the Revolution of 1911, also known as the Xinhai Revolution, the latter named because of the year it took place in (1911 was known as the year of the Xinhai in the Chinese calendar, which means "metal pig"). The pressure came to a head during 1911 when a military revolt erupted in the province of Wuhan, known as the Wuchang uprising. Discontent with the dynastic rule, coupled with the recent famine, caused many people to join the Xinhai Revolution. The rapid spread of revolution led to the Qing emperor's formal abdication about a year later in 1912 and to the establishment of the Republic of China.

Whether Mao fought or not in this anti-dynastic revolution is debated, with some sources saying that he participated in a single battle and others saying he merely supported the anti-Qing perspective. It is possible that he did participate in the skirmishes, but considering the cult of personality that would rise around him later, it is equally likely that he did not participate and that it was later claimed that he had a more active role in creating a new order that ended the "oppressive" dynasty rule. Mao did serve as a soldier during this time, which furthered his childhood admiration for the military and for the people in charge of the army.

As the nation began to be reshaped, Mao became a librarian and then a school principal. During this time, he was a prolific reader, focusing on books about power, government, and history. His reading included many works on Chinese literature and history, as well as *The Communist Manifesto*, which was originally Karl Marx's *Manifesto of the Communist Party*. Mao did read other works on government, but this book may have had the most effect on him since there was a living example of it unfolding in Russia around that time. He was also said to have been enamored with other notable Western military leaders, like George Washington of the United States and Napoleon Bonaparte of France.

In 1919, Mao went to Beijing as demonstrations of the May Fourth Movement were beginning. After World War I, the Republic of China had thought that the defeat of the Germans and their allies would result in the restoration of the Shandong Province, which had been taken from China in 1898 and had been a German territory. Instead, the Allies acknowledged this territory as being a part of Japan. During the May Fourth Movement, students protested the Treaty of Versailles, which ended World War I and ignored the Chinese claim to the territory. This grew into greater discontent, as the changes that had been expected to follow the end of the Revolution of 1911 had not been realized. The people began to believe that all the revolution had accomplished was a regime change, not the real change that was needed to help the people. During this time, Mao began to write articles that he published in local journals, calling for cultural reforms and talking about how there was a growth of a new culture within the country.

Involvement in the Chinese Communist Party

By 1920, Mao had returned to his home province, Hunan, where he began to be more active in forwarding the ideas of communism. Sometime in 1920, he married Yang Kaihui. In 1921, Chinese radicals began to form a vision for the country based on the tenants of Marxism and Leninism instead of the ideals of capitalism and liberalism that the nations that made up the Allies believed in. Their solution ended up being the founding of the Chinese Communist Party (CPC). Part of the change they enacted was in a shift in language, using less formal and more colloquial speech to make the ideas more accessible to the people.

With this new cultural and ideological shift, the youth of China began to take a more prominent role in shaping the future of the nation. This would no doubt help form Mao's own ideas of the best way to enact change later on. At the time, he was still relatively young, but he was nearly thirty years old, and when compared to the college students and young adults who were joining the CPC, he was on the older side.

Mao joined the first CPC Congress in 1921. Taking the ideas from the meeting, he began to organize and implement the party within Hunan, where he lived during this time. Using his skills from his time teaching and writing during the revolution a decade earlier, Mao wrote essays for Changsha's newspapers. Working off the ideas from the May Fourth Movement, he injected Marxist ideology and communist beliefs into the existing ideologies that had already been espoused.

Mao was mainly focused on helping the workers, which resulted in the formation of at least twenty unions that he controlled. Unions were formed for many of the primary industries, including the railways, mining, and textiles. Mao also sought to educate peasants who did not have the opportunity to learn, and he provided classes in mathematics and reading. While these classes served the functional purpose of educating people, it also came with an ulterior motive—it gave Mao a way of beginning to promote communist ideas and indoctrinate a large group of people. It helped to bring more people into the CPC, quickly raising the number of CPC members within Hunan and increase Mao's own importance within the CPC.

Mao Zedong was able to reap these benefits as he was voted to be a member of the Central Committee of the CPC in 1923. He also joined the Kuomintang (KMT, also known as the Chinese Nationalist Party) that year. The KMT tasked members of the CPC with trying to bring the Republic of China a nationalist government, which Mao had been doing since he had joined the CPC. To better perform his duties, he moved to Shanghai, where he was further elevated the next year to run the nationalist propaganda bureau. For the next few years, Mao worked to bring the two parties closer together since they both had similar interests and visions for the nation.

At the beginning of 1924, he lived with his wife, Yang Kaihui, and their two sons in Shanghai, the capital of China. This arrangement made it easier for him to participate as one of the leaders of the Nationalists' Executive Bureau. By the end of the year, though, he needed a break. Returning to his home province, Mao noticed the amount of unrest among the peasants of Shaoshan, a city in Hunan. Following the shooting of more than two dozen Chinese peasants in Shanghai, the peasants were beginning to revolt, which further inspired Mao's thoughts on their potential to engage in revolution.

Though he had come from a peasant family himself, Mao had largely turned his back on his family during his late teen years. After more than a decade away from his family, he had adopted the thoughts and views of intellectuals, considering himself to be one of those intellectuals instead of a peasant. Mao had adopted a similar perception of them that Marx held; mainly, he had contempt for their lack of education, considering them to be backward. This is perhaps exacerbated by his roots being in the peasant class, as he would seek to distance himself from them and only use them to expand his own power. As he would demonstrate during the Cultural Revolution, Mao preferred to keep the peasants oppressed when he did think of them at all.

Seeing their unrest and growing action against the wrongs done against them, Mao saw the potential to harness their unrest and expand his own power within the country. Their protests became a means of networking and organizing the people under his cause.

When the leader of the KMT, Sun Yat-sen, died in 1925, the new leader began to split the KMT from the CPC. Instead of supporting each other, the new leader of the KMT, Chiang Kai-shek, felt threatened by the CPC. As a result, Chiang ordered a massacre in the capital city of Shanghai, resulting in the death of many communists and members of the CPC.

Mao had seen his role in the coalition significantly reduced in 1925, but now he had a reason to fear for his life. During the fall of 1927, the Chinese Civil War began. The CPC ordered Mao to begin a peasant uprising that would harm the KMT that controlled the region. The peasants did not stand a chance. Upon their failure, Mao went into hiding in the Jiangxi province, which bordered on the eastern side of Hunan. With little way to contact other CPC members and having to hide in the mountains, Mao made use of the time he was given to train the peasants in warfare. After training them in guerrilla tactics for about a year, he and his military were far more capable of posing a threat when they finally emerged from hiding in 1929. Meeting with other CPC leaders, Mao and his group established a basis for their party in Jiangxi.

Prelude to WWII: Power Struggle between the CPC and KMT, and Japanese Intervention

During 1931, the KMT started a campaign that was designed to completely eradicate all the communists from the country. As the two parties began to have more serious conflicts, the Japanese military saw an opportunity to take more lands that were claimed by the Chinese. By planting a bomb on a Manchurian railway, the Japanese military created a scenario in which it looked like the Chinese Civil War was affecting other nations. Following the bombing, Japan claimed the area after a successful invasion.

Tired from four years of attacks by the KMT and realizing their own vulnerability to other outside threats, the CPC decided to relocate to a more secure area in 1934. It was reported that roughly 80,000 loyal CPC members left Jiangxi to look for a new base. After three months of seeking a new home, Mao Zedong took control over the Red Army, the forces of the CPC. As Japan expanded into Chinese territories on the eastern side of the country and as the KMT tried to wipe out the CPC farther inland and toward the middle of the country, the men had to march far to the west and then north to escape persecution from both sides. By the time they finally reached the safer areas of China, they had crossed more than 6,000 miles, which included traversing over mountains. This became known as the Long March. It is uncertain how many men actually set out at the beginning and how many survived, as they did not keep detailed records of the personnel involved. There is a wide gap in how many people historians believe died on the march, with some estimating it at 10,000, while others say it was closer to 70,000. What is known for sure is that the CPC finally had a chance to consider their next move after finally reaching the north-central province of Shaanxi in 1935.

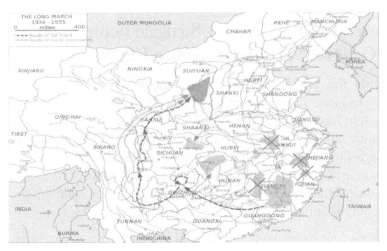

Route of the Long March from Jiangxi to Shaanxi

The majority of the people in China had lost interest in which party was in control since they considered the Japanese to be of much greater concern. The sentiment against internal strife had been growing since the Japanese had invaded in 1931. By 1936, even the CPC and KMT finally decided that their greatest enemy was not the other party but the invading outsiders who continued to chip away at Chinese territories. Though this sentiment was growing within both parties, the leaders did not seem quite as understanding. It took one of the KMT officers abducting the KMT leader, Chiang Kai-shek, to finally force the leaders of the parties to work together to remove the growing Japanese threat. Known as the Xi'an Incident, it was only resolved when the KMT and CPC finally formed a tense alliance, which was called the Second United Front.

The timing could not have been better for the Chinese people, as Japan finally let their real intentions be known in 1937. After launching a full invasion, the Second Sino-Japanese War finally began. The Japanese invaders were brutal, and their successful attacks on the northern portions of the country became infamous. Having captured the KMT's capital of Nanjing, the Japanese committed numerous crimes against humanity, resulting in what came to be known as the Rape of Nanjing, also written as the Rape of Nanking. The invaders faced greater resistance when they tried to push into Shaanxi, though, and the CPC resistance stopped them from progressing farther west.

Around 1943, a new position was created within the CPC, chairman of the Communist Central Committee. Mao was given the new title, as well as being made the chairman of the Politburo, the executive committee that determined the direction the government and country would take. This made him the sole leader of the Communist Party of China as they fought to remove the Japanese from China.

When the US decimated the Japanese cities of Hiroshima (August 6th, 1945) and Nagasaki (August 9th, 1945), signaling the end of World War II, the Japanese withdrew from the Republic of China. Without a reason to band together, both the KMT and CPC resumed their war to control China within a year after the Japanese left.

Post-WWII China: Return to Civil War

In 1947, the KMT finally managed to do what the Japanese hadn't: they captured Mao's base in Yan'an, which was established after the end of the Long March. By this time, though, the CPC had already created a new base for their operations in Manchuria. They had selected this region because Russia had a presence nearby, and the CPC and Russia had allied together because of their desire to further a theoretical communist government in their respective countries.

Feeling more confident with their new allies nearby, the CPC became more aggressive against their old nemesis, the KMT. This confidence proved to be well-founded as the CPC finally defeated the KMT in 1949. The remnants of the KMT fled to Taiwan by the end of the year, leaving continental China in the hands of the CPC.

Mainland China and Taiwan

Seeing a way of rebranding a name that was associated with division, Mao declared the new government to be the People's Republic of China on October 1ˢᵗ, 1949. A few months later, from Taiwan, Chiang Kai-shek, who had been the chairman of the Republic of China and the leader of the KMT, declared themselves to be the legitimate government, and they proclaimed Taipei to be the capital of the Republic of China. In 1950, Chiang became the president of the Republic of China, a position that he held until 1975. The division between these two parties still exists today, with mainland China claiming the large island of Taiwan as a Chinese territory, even though the Republic of China is still based in Taiwan.

Many nations consider there to be one sovereign state under the name of China since both states use "China" in their names; this is known as the One-China Policy. This is not the same as the One-China Principle, which is the People's Republic of China's view on the matter, as the One-China Principle states that they are both a single entity. There are times when the Republic of China actually concurs with this principle; however, they differ in opinion on who is in control since both the government of mainland China and the government of Taiwan claim to be the legitimate government. It is a similar situation to the divisions in North and South Korea or the more modern example of the Syrian government and its opposition at the beginning of the 21st century.

Chapter 2 – The Suspicion Behind the United Face

Mao Zedong and the CPC had formed a close relationship with the Soviet Union by the end of the 1940s. It was in Joseph Stalin's best interest to have a large ally to the eastern border of the USSR, although there were also indications that he was less than pleased with the idea of Mao and the CPC being the leaders of the new Chinese government.

The Soviet Role in Mao's Victory

Prior to the successful defeat of the KMT, Mao and the CPC had been in dire straits because of the erosion of their resources. The early successes of the KMT made it seem less likely that the CPC would be any more successful this time around than they had been prior to the Second Sino-Japanese War. Ultimately, it was the CPC's alliance with Russia that resulted in the CPC taking control of the mainland.

Mao and Stalin actually had direct communications with each other, with Stalin actively pressuring Mao to act against both the KMT and the growing influence of the Western countries in the region. In an effort to spur Mao into action, Stalin warned Mao that the West would work together to undermine the CPC. He pointed to the close proximity of the British, claiming that Great Britain had the ability to "activate the Muslims," who lived in the Xinjiang region. Stalin further warned that the West would destabilize Mao's position in 1949, and he pressured Mao and the CPC to act.

Although he was planning to invade Xinjiang in 1950, Mao knew that he did not have the necessary resources or ability to travel with his men. In September 1949, he sent a communication to Stalin, letting the Soviet leader know that the CPC was not equipped to attack the province and requested assistance. Mao had managed to persuade Stalin to send aid by saying that without it, he would be unable to strike before the spring of 1950. The worst-case scenario he presented to the USSR leader was having to wait until 1951 to attack those opposing the Communist Party. Stalin readily agreed and sent airplanes to help move the troops, as the railways and other means of transportation available to the Chinese would have hindered the CPC from acting as soon as possible. Mao also requested other resources, such as food and fuel, which Stalin provided to ensure that Mao and the Communist Party would be able to succeed. With the extra supplies, the Communist Party was able to strike ahead of the timeline that Mao had planned. Instead of invading in 1950, the party was able to strike in October 1949. Since no one had expected the Communist Party to recover so quickly, the Nationalist Party was not prepared for the quick attack made possible by Stalin's assistance.

Without this alliance, the CPC would not have gained the upper hand so quickly or perhaps at all. It is difficult to say what would have happened without Stalin's interference on the side of the CPC. Both parties of China were depleted, and the country was already facing serious financial and resource problems soon after the end of the Second Sino-Japanese War.

In return for his aid, Stalin received updates directly from Mao so that he knew of the CPC's successes soon after they occurred. It is not entirely known what benefits Stalin sought from this support beyond expanding communism and having the leader of the new regime of China owing favors to the Soviet Union.

How the Two Communist Countries Looked from the Outside and the Problems That They Hid

To many people in the West, the relationship between Stalin and Mao seemed to be strong. They had a common border that stretched more than 2,000 miles, which gave them the appearance of being closely tied together both in location and in ideology. It appeared that these two countries were positioned to change the dynamic of Asia, posing a threat as far west as India and Iran.

This appeared to be confirmed when the Korean War began in 1950. The CPC had only recently taken control of China at the end of 1949, and they were already working with the Soviets to help another rising communist government in Korea. Kim Il-sung was the leader of the Democratic People's Republic of Korea, which he had established in 1948, and he had previously supported the Soviets, who had occupied regions around them during the Second Sino-Japanese War. Japan had gained control over the peninsula after the First Sino-Japanese War ended in 1895 and had made Korea a Japanese colony. When the Japanese were defeated in World War II in 1945, the Soviets moved into the region and began occupying the northern portion of the peninsula, an area that had been part of the Russian tsar's lands. Following the end of World War II, the US had decided to arbitrarily divide the nation of Korea along the 38th parallel, without having discussed any of the potential problems, repercussions, or risks with anyone knowledgeable about the country. The top portion would be communist under the supervision of the Soviet Union, while the lower portion would be under US leadership.

The US was not completely prepared to deal with the newly established country of South Korea. Many of the South Koreans despised the US presence, as they had just been freed from 35 years of Japanese rule and now had another foreign country intervening in their affairs. And to be fair, they had a right to be upset. The US had supported the Japanese government in Korea, allowed the former Japanese governors to stay on as advisors after World War II, and supported the United Nations elections that ultimately split the country in two, something that many Koreans resented. They were also unfamiliar with the language and the political climate of the country, leading them to make decisions that further destabilized the country.

The agreement had been that the USSR and the US would help to reunite the country in 1948, an agreement that neither side was willing to honor when the time came. So, in 1950, the leader of North Korea, Kim Il-sung, sought to reunify the peninsula under his communist rule. Having left South Korea in the hands of Syngman Rhee, the president of the First Republic of Korea, in 1949, the US again took an interest in the country, as they feared the spread of communism. When Kim Il-sung invaded South Korea, the United Nations sent in troops to stop the incursion, with the US sending a large force to keep the Korean leader from succeeding. China and the USSR both sent their own troops to help support North Korea. Mao feared capitalism would take root on the mainland, while Stalin largely provided money and technical assistance. Wary of getting involved in the war, Mao sent a small contingent of men, with 282 reported causalities, to help unite the peninsula. When the UN began sending forces in support of South Korea, Mao seemed to back off from helping North Korea, though he was vocal about his opposition to any peace settlement in the region. Stalin died in 1953, and the war ended almost five months later, resulting in the two very different Koreas that still exist more almost seventy years later.

Mao's Wariness and Separation from Stalin's Memory

Despite the aid that Stalin had provided the CPC, he and Mao had a contentious relationship. Perhaps one of the best sources for their difference of opinions was stated by Mao himself during 1962:

> In 1945, Stalin wanted to prevent China from making revolution, saying that we should not have a civil war and should cooperate with Chiang Kai-shek, otherwise the Chinese nation would perish. But we did not do what he said. The revolution was victorious. After the victory of the revolution he next suspected China of being a Yugoslavia, and that I would become a second Tito.

> - *Mao Zedong*

It is possible, even probable, that Stalin was initially resistant to providing aid for the Chinese Civil War. Backing either side could potentially backfire, as it later would, though Stalin would not live long enough to see that he had been right to be wary of Mao. In 1945, World War II had left few nations unaffected. Stalin knew that the Western world was already against him and that it would be a greater benefit for him to have a party that was sympathetic to communism as one of the leading parties of the country of China than if the KMT had completely wiped out the CPC.

However, when it became clear that Mao would not heed Stalin's advice to work with Chiang Kai-shek, it was probably obvious to the Soviet leader which side was of greater benefit as an ally. This was why Stalin decided to back the Communist Party, even though he had reservations about Mao and the party. By the time Mao made the above statement, though, Stalin was dead. Without his ally there to contradict him, Mao was able to make it sound like he and the CPC were able to successfully win against the KMT while the whole world was against them. He minimized the role that the Soviets played, even though the war would certainly have lasted longer without Soviet intervention—it is even possible that Mao and his party would have failed to remove the opposition completely. After all, it was the element of surprise that had led to the quick victory, and that was only possible because Stalin sent planes and supplies to move soldiers quickly. Ironically, this statement proved that Mao was exactly what he was declaring himself to be, something that Stalin feared.

It is perhaps best that Stalin did not live to see his fears realized about China. The fledgling relationship with Mao and the CPC was never a stable one, with mistrust present on both sides. The foundation was shaky at best, and Stalin's paranoia likely would have caused more issues over time. However, in March of 1953, Stalin died, and his work to build a stable relationship with the new Chinese government would quickly fall apart. As Soviet leadership passed on to others, they would begin to implement their own agendas. Even though the trust between Stalin and Mao was always fragile, there was a respect between the two leaders. Stalin had chosen to support Mao, and Mao respected Stalin's ability to push a nation in a direction that the Chinese leader felt was close to Lenin's ideas. This would not be the case with the Soviet leaders who followed, and this could have been part of the reason for Mao's minimalization of the Soviet Union's role. It may have been a way of ensuring that the new Soviet leadership did not try to use their assistance as leverage against China.

As can be seen, while the relationship between the People's Republic of China and the Soviet Union appeared to the outside world to be unified, the cracks were always there. It was just that the tyrants were far more adept at hiding these problems to present that united front because they really had to rely on themselves since democracy and capitalism were being spread over much of the rest of the world.

Chapter 3 – The Five-Year Plan, the Great Leap Forward, and the Events Leading to the Cultural Revolution

After the victory of the CPC in 1949 to take control over China, the nation was in a very difficult situation, both economically and culturally. The Second Sino-Japanese War had merely been a break in the Chinese Civil War, meaning the nation had continuously been at war for nearly a quarter of a century. And war can tend to bring out the worst of humanity. Even when the Japanese invaded China and the CPC and KMT agreed to quit fighting with each other, they did little to actually work together as a unit to dispel the Japanese. Both sides were also as cruel as the invaders to the people of China, disregarding the lives of the peasants as each one tried to root out their opposition.

The rise of Mao could have been a real change for the people of China. For the first time since 1927, they finally had peace. Unfortunately, though, Mao's vision for China had no place for dissidents, as he followed a similar trajectory that Stalin took once he controlled the country. The Cultural Revolution was Mao's final attempt to cement his legacy and ensure that his vision of China continued after his death.

After Stalin's Death

The Soviet Union underwent a couple of years of uncertainty following Stalin's death on March 5th, 1953. Nikita Khrushchev not only managed to survive under Stalin, but he also navigated his way to the top, managing to engineer the execution of Lavrentiy Beria (the state security chief under Stalin) in 1953 and besting the man who was Stalin's heir apparent, Georgy Malenkov, by 1955. By the time the 20th Congress of the Communist Party of the Soviet Union was held in February of 1956, Khrushchev had garnished a considerable amount of attention within the party. At the time, Khrushchev was the first secretary of the Communist Party of the Soviet Union (CPSU), making him an incredibly powerful man. During the meeting, he gave what has come to be known as the "Secret Speech," in which he was incredibly critical of the late Soviet leader. In his speech, Khrushchev said that Stalin's "intolerance, his brutality, his abuse of power," had harmed the country.

His criticism of Stalin's behavior was shocking, but he did not stop at simply saying that the late leader's behavior had been wrong. Khrushchev went on to illustrate how detrimental Stalin's policies had been, saying that the Great Purge that Stalin had initiated in the 1930s had been wrong, as had the drive to silence anyone who spoke out against him. The discussion of these atrocities could have been problematic, not only because of how many people had participated in those atrocities but because they had also been conditioned for more than twenty years not to question it. Now with the grievances against Stalin finally being voiced, a kind of thaw developed that allowed people to feel like they could speak their minds. As a result of Khrushchev's speech, millions of people who had been imprisoned based on political grounds were released, and the government acknowledged that many of the 750,000 people who were executed during the Great Purge had not been guilty of whatever they had been charged with.

Many of the complaints that Khrushchev had voiced in Moscow Mao had already considered. Stalin's reputation had come at a high cost, and Mao knew that he could use the perception of Stalin and the oppression that had resulted from it to his own advantage. In 1956, Mao gave his own speech that has come to be known as his "Hundred Flowers" address. In this speech, Mao wanted to give the intellectuals a way of expressing themselves so that they would feel like they had a say in the direction that the nation was going to take. Up to that point, Mao's focus had been on the peasants and those of lower birth. This was the first time where he seemed to seek input and opinions from an upper class of China, and he encouraged open discussion of what could be done differently or better. Mao had not shown any such willingness for discourse since the May Fourth Movement, but this speech provided justification for a more open path of communication, indicating that he was not going to be like Stalin. Mao's speech included the idea that what China needed was to "let a hundred flowers bloom, let a hundred schools of thought contend."

As Nikita Khrushchev rose to power, taking control of the party in 1956, the Russians began to see a lot more freedom given to thoughts and ideas that did not necessarily agree with Khrushchev's own. Mao's intentions, however, were entirely different. He did not seek to encourage free thought; those who spoke up to voice their opposition or disagreement with Mao were rounded up and were imprisoned or killed. His sole desire in speaking ill of Stalin was to draw out dissent. It is possible that Mao had not expected the kind of reactions he received, and he may have even wanted to have other ideas mix with his own originally. It is true that he had ignored the recommendations of some of his advisors who said that this speech could harm them. They pointed to how the relaxed control under Khrushchev had resulted in revolutions in both Poland and Hungary; Khrushchev was even nearly removed from power in 1957.

However, when the intellectuals began to question Mao himself, the reaction was quick, although he certainly should have expected it, considering how much he had criticized Stalin. Whether he felt they had betrayed his intentions of trying to give them a voice, or if he had always planned to use the speech to weed out as many dissenters as possible, by 1957, Mao had largely removed anyone who expressed opposition to his vision of a communist China.

The Five-Year Plan

To quickly recap, China was still reeling from the economic problems of more than two decades of war. Following the founding of the People's Republic of China in 1949, the government had to consolidate and gain control over the entire country while working to remove any KMT remnants from the mainland. China joined in the Korean War, further harming its own financial situation. For the next few years, China tried to recover from the economic turmoil, and during this time, Mao and the other party leaders sought to draft a more concrete path to recovery.

The end result was the First Five-Year Plan.

The plan began in 1953 and was planned to end in 1957. The primary focus of the First Five-Year Plan was to stimulate a high rate of growth. This would be accomplished in part by initiating a change from the agrarian economy, which China had historically been, to one that was built more on heavy industries and technology. Knowing that such a large change would not be possible overnight, the First Five-Year Plan set goals so that Mao and other government officials could evaluate the success of the plan and determine how to best move forward.

The First Five-Year Plan closely followed what Stalin had done in working to industrialize the USSR, as it was clear that that was the only way to become the world leader that Mao wanted China to be. To do this, the Chinese government had to heavily invest in the necessary facilities, education, and tools. They also opted to follow the plans that the Soviets had used to quickly remodel their society and ownership. This meant further reliance on the Soviets to help draft the plan to expedite these changes. Among the changes, farmers and those who worked the fields were formed into collectives. The state now owned much of the land and held the reins to all future economic spending and planning.

After the plan began, China quickly found itself facing many problems that it had not anticipated. By the end of the First Five-year Plan in 1957, it was apparent that the Soviet model would not work in the much more agrarian China. They were even further behind the technologies of the time than the Russians had been. It did not help that they had a problem to face that Russia did not, as China had many more people to look over than the USSR did. Since the government of the People's Republic of China faced unique problems to their country, the solutions to them could not be modeled after the methods used by the Soviets.

To succeed in their vision for China, the government realized that they needed to have a much larger scale of national industrialization. The USSR was willing to help China accomplish this, but they only agreed to provide financial aid through loans that would have to be repaid at set times. This meant that the Chinese government needed to convert all of its financial institutions and businesses into state-operated endeavors. Both credit policies and the nation's taxes were rewritten to strongly discourage businesses from being run as private companies, and when the First Five-Year Plan ended, there were no longer any private companies within the entire country.

The methods that the government used to industrialize the country more rapidly were successful, though. They saw a significant increase in the production of heavy industry products, such as cement and metals. From the time the plan started until its end in 1957, China saw a nineteen percent annual increase in industrial products, as well as a nine percent increase in how much workers earned.

Given the enormous population of the nation, agriculture needed to be modernized so that more workers could begin working in industrial positions. Since the government had established collectives, they had complete control over how much farmers could charge for the food. This would prove to cause another serious problem later, but at this time, the government did not think of the future of agriculture in terms of anything other than how it was necessary to further the industrial and business industries. The farmers and their families who were forced to join the collectives were still able to have small plots of land for themselves and the production of their own food.

Khrushchev recognized the importance of China as an ally, though he was not yet in charge of the Soviet Union when China's First Five-Year Plan began. At that time, he was the USSR's first secretary, so he did have quite a bit of sway over the direction of the USSR. While he was not willing (or able) to give China the necessary money without repayment, he did want to strengthen the bonds that had been developed between Mao and Stalin. Khrushchev was able to accomplish this by renegotiating trade deals that had been established under Stalin that he considered to be unfair to the Chinese. During the early days of China's industrialization, the USSR was one of their primary trade collaborators. By 1955, an estimated sixty percent of China's exports were sent to the USSR.

The duration of the First Five-Year Plan is considered to be a golden age for both sides, as it was the best period for Sino-Soviet relations. However, the problems were already starting to form as both men disliked the other. When Khrushchev made his "Secret Speech," it put Mao in a very difficult position. Despite having worked to minimize Stalin's role in his rise to power, Mao had been vocally supportive of the late leader's ideas and methods. It is possible that the "Hundred Flowers" speech was Mao's attempt to move China in a similar direction as the Soviet Union, considering the close bond that the USSR and China had made since Stalin's death. However, once that proved to be a terrible move for the party leaders, Mao and Khrushchev took different paths in moving the ideals of communism forward.

As such, tensions continued to mount, and when the USSR sided with the Tibetan rebels who rose up against China in 1959, the split between the two countries became too great for them to ultimately overcome. Private arguments and complaints became public in 1960, with Mao and Khrushchev openly insulting each other. Some attempts were made to heal the divisions between the nations, but neither leader was willing to budge or forgive, resulting in a complete split in 1962. When Khrushchev signed the Limited Test Ban Treaty with the US and Great Britain, Mao took it as an open attempt by the three countries to hinder China's own nuclear advancements. Between 1963 and 1964, Mao penned nine letters, which he published, that stated everything he saw as wrong or bad about Khrushchev's leadership abilities.

Another problem that Mao likely had with what transpired following the "Secret Speech" was that Stalin's legacy was so quickly undermined, with the next long-term leader of the USSR significantly changing the vision of what communism meant for the country. It was an early warning sign to Mao of what could happen in China after his death, and it was a lesson he would not forget in his old age.

The Great Leap Forward

Over the span of three years, from 1958 to 1961, Mao and the Chinese government forced millions of people who had lived on farms into communes in what is known as the Great Leap Forward. This was an economic and social movement to transform China into a communist society by moving away from an agrarian economy. Some of these communes were farm cooperatives, where the people were able to continue using many of their existing knowledge and skills. Other people were sent to places where they would learn how to perform manufacturing tasks and activities. People living in these communes were expected to complete their assigned tasks, which meant there were people who moved into completely different fields than agriculture and manufacturing. For example, there were people who were dedicated to raising the children of the communes, which meant that children mainly lived in centers where those assigned to childcare largely raised them. All of the regular chores were collectivized, and people were expected to do their share, in addition to whatever work the government assigned them, to support the primary function of the collective.

Mao changed the way farming was done, basing the new approach on the methods used in the USSR. Most of these methods were not scientifically correct, however. For example, the Soviet ideas stated that plants needed to support each other, so they were grown close together, often forcing the plants to compete for the same nutrients and light. Another method involved plowing the fields several feet (sometimes as much as six feet) deep under the false idea that it would encourage the plants to develop better roots. The results of these methods were detrimental to the people since it completely ruined entire crops, meaning that a lot less food was produced in the first year. Future crop yields were damaged because the deep trenches that resulted from the plowing significantly harmed the fields.

In an effort to increase how much metal the country produced (thereby reducing how much they would need to import), Mao initially encouraged people to establish their own furnaces where scrap metal could be turned into steel. This encouragement quickly evolved into a demand, forcing families to meet a set quota. Instead of using scrap metal, families and collectives ended up having to melt down useful items that they still used to keep from falling behind their quotas. It also resulted in the destruction of large portions of forests, as communities had to build the furnaces on lands that were not currently being used for other needs. With the loss of forests and the new destructive farming methods, the once fertile fields of China were left drained of their nutrients and became far more vulnerable to erosion.

None of these problems were obvious during the first year of the Great Leap Forward, though. 1958 saw an especially productive harvest because neither the fields nor the forests had yet been seriously affected by the implemented changes. Unfortunately, so many people had moved from the farms to the manufacturing collectives that there were not enough people to harvest the bumper crops, resulting in a lot of waste. Good food rotted in the fields, and so, people living in the cities and manufacturing collectives did not see any increase in food.

The problem was further exacerbated when the leaders of many of the communes lied about how much they had been able to harvest. Officials arrived to take the food for other communes and cities based on calculations of what was needed there. Since the government used false numbers to determine how much would be left over, many of the agriculture communes did not have sufficient food left for their own people. Over the next year, starvation began to rise in the agriculture communes.

When the Yellow River flooded in 1959, it proved to be disastrous. While this was a natural occurrence, it compounded the problems caused by the changes to the farming system. An estimated two million people died as a result of drowning in the floods or from starvation. Then, in 1960, a drought struck portions of China.

The majority of deaths from this time were from starvation in the urban areas of the country. The current official number of dead is said to be fourteen million people, but few scholars agree with this number. By the time the government was able to start recovering from the damages, historians estimate that the death toll was between 20 and 48 million people, though the actual number of people who perished will most likely never be known.

This period was supposed to be the Second Five-Year Plan, but it was so disastrous that Mao stopped its implementation in 1961, a year before it should have ended. Those three years are now often referred to as China's "Three Bitter Years," as they are among some of the most tragic events in modern history.

Because he had been the primary driver behind the Great Leap Forward, Mao was essentially removed from his position, although he still kept his title as chairman of the CPC. He would not gain the same level of control over China until 1966 with the beginning of the Cultural Revolution. When he again gained control, Mao would seek to ensure his legacy with an iron fist.

Chapter 4 – Fighting the Capitalism of the West

The breakdown in relations between the Soviet Union and China exposed a serious problem with communism on how it was practiced on a large scale: there were just too many different competing ideas on how it should be enacted. Just like smaller countries, such as Cuba and Vietnam, China and the USSR were forced to choose which type of communism was best for their countries. Looking at the events of what happened, there was no form of communism that actually followed Marx's ideals or tenants. All of the communist leaders were tyrants who demanded loyalty, much as Adolf Hitler had done during the rise of the Nazi Party in the 1920s and 1930s.

Communist leaders claimed power under the guise of wanting what was best for the people of the country. By stoking fear and pitting classes against each other, these communist leaders were forced to rule with an iron fist. Similar issues can easily be associated with democracies and republics, as history has repeatedly proven. During the 20th century, communism was still new, so its implementation and the possibilities for abuse were much greater. This was what led to such a schism between the two large communist countries.

When the Cultural Revolution began, Mao Zedong feared that a revisionist approach to Marx's methods was what had destroyed the communist order in the Soviet Union (though, to be fair, his relationship with Stalin had also been very contentious). While the change in Soviet communism concerned him, in 1966, it was capitalism that became the larger threat.

A Growing Fear of Revisionism

To China, the Soviet's changes following Stalin's death was a blatant example of revisionism. Today, revisionism is seen as a sign of weakness, indecisiveness, or failure, and this was largely how Mao viewed the events occurring in the Soviet Union. Mao certainly used the term revisionism in a negative context (and many nations still use it in the same way). To Mao, the direction that Nikita Khrushchev was taking the Soviet Union in was a revision of the direction that Stalin had taken. They were undermining the purpose of communism to benefit those who had survived Stalin and risen to the top.

Mao was undoubtedly acting in his own interests, but to some extent, he was concerned about the people of China. The policies under State Chairman Liu Shaoqi and General Secretary Deng Xiaoping had stabilized the country, but there were some classes that had improved quicker than others. From a more objective position, that was inevitable, as the people at the top of a government rarely feel the same hardships as the lower classes do, and by the time they do, they are already working to correct it. For example, only Mao's pride and level of power in the CPC suffered due to the disastrous Great Leap Forward. He did not have to worry about starvation or drowning the way other people did. Nor was he uprooted to live in a collective that was not equipped to handle the people who were moved to it. Mao was safe from the worst effects of the policies that he had helped to establish.

To Mao, the actions of Liu and Deng were the beginning of a revisionist history in China while he was still alive. The people who benefited most from the new policies seemed more like capitalists, as the new changes seemed more closely aligned with the capitalist world than it did with communism.

The Elitist Capitalism of the West

One of the greatest fears that Mao held was that China was moving toward capitalism, and Mao's fears were not entirely unfounded. While the Soviet Union was still communist, the 1990s would show that they had been moving toward capitalism for decades. Having fought for communism since the 1920s, Mao likely saw the utopia he had envisioned slipping away after his death.

Mao best expressed his fears for the future in 1963, stating that if "the landlords, rich peasants, counter-revolutionaries, bad elements, and monsters are all allowed to crawl out...then it will not be long before a counter-revolutionary restoration on a national scale inevitably occurred, the Marxist-Leninist party would undoubtedly become a revisionist party or a fascist party." To Mao, capitalism was built on a hierarchy that generally kept a large percentage of the people at the bottom while lifting up the few. Once a person or family reached the top, they would retain power and oppress others. Mao wanted to ensure that all of the people in China had comparable lives, ignoring the fact that his social structure was fairly similar to that of a capitalist country; it was just the means of staying in power that differed. To keep power, Mao would not use money or manipulation of the system. Instead, he would use persecution and violence to stop dissenters from warping the communist utopia he envisioned.

In addition to his mistrust of capitalism and those who practiced it, Mao was an atheist since all major world religions had developed hierarchies, which could be easily compared to the social structures in capitalist nations. He was also against the kinds of superstitions of the past that could possibly hinder progress. In an act that would likely enrage Mao today, shrines and temples have been allowed to form across China, particularly in recent years.

While it is easy to look back and find fault with Mao and the communist leaders for their tight control over their people, the capitalist nations were also not entirely innocent. The strong reaction against the spread of communism was often violent, as seen by the Korean and Vietnam Wars, as well as in the many proxy wars that took place in countries like Cuba and Afghanistan. Nor were the events within capitalist countries benign. During the 1950s, while Mao was implementing the First Five-Year Plan and the Great Leap Forward, McCarthyism was spreading across the United States. American politicians were actively cracking down on people in power and the media, and they unjustly imprisoned political leaders and celebrities based on the suspicion that those leaders and celebrities were communist sympathizers. Anyone who spoke out against Senator Joseph McCarthy or the Republicans who were oppressing an entire nation, although their focus was mainly on those with power or had a large platform from which to espouse ideas, could be jailed. Leading members of the media, such as Edward R. Murrow, a man who had been a key American reporter during World War II, were intimidated to keep them from speaking out against what was going on in the country. All of this was clearly against the First Amendment, which guarantees free speech. Yet for several years, the US was held in the grip of a different kind of tyranny that also claimed to be for the good of the people.

The extreme vilification of China and communism in the US had kept these two countries from having any meaningful discussion for decades. It wouldn't be until February 1972 that the US and China would finally begin to have open discussions about their respective futures.

Chapter 5 – The Introduction of Revolution

From 1960 until 1966, Mao had largely been sidelined. During his time controlling the direction of the country, the relationship between China and the USSR had completely broken down, and millions of Chinese had died because of the Second Five-Year Plan. During the six years when he was largely a side character in the government that he had founded, Mao had time to analyze the direction that China was going in and to calculate his next move. All he needed was a way to regain control over the government.

Mao's Return to Power

Liu Shaoqi, who became the second chairman of the People's Republic of China in 1959, and Deng Xiaoping strove to undo the combined damage of the natural disasters and destructive agrarian practices. The extreme tactics of the Great Leap Forward gave way to more measured approaches that more closely mirrored some of the aspects of the changes of the Soviet Union since Stalin's death. Of greater concern to Mao, though, was the change in the agricultural system. The collectives that he had established had begun to fall apart, and in some places, the collectives had entirely dissolved, and private farms had resumed. There was also a similar thaw in the approach to different art forms, including literature, something that he had suppressed as much as possible. He did not want people to have access to the kinds of material that had helped to influence him. Without Mao in power, literature wasn't exactly encouraged, but the dual leadership did not actively work against the arts. However, their focus was elsewhere as they had to repair the damage done under Mao and his overzealous, unrealistic move to implement communism according to his ideals. This meant restructuring how everything was managed, in part because so many of the communes had fallen apart. Liu and Deng had changed the focus so that management received more control, and workers were now rewarded based on their individual efforts instead of the workers being the main driver.

members of this organization began to be brought into the government, they had more sway, and it further elevated the People Liberation Army's role in the nation, as Mao pointed to them as a great example of how the people of China should be.

The Announcement and the Beginning

Believing that the country was going in the wrong direction, Mao wanted to strengthen the ideology that had brought his party to power seventeen years earlier. Even though the people who supported Mao had been working through the crises caused by the Great Leap Forward, the leaders seemed to have moved the direction of the country away from his intended vision, and Mao possibly felt that he had been betrayed. To ensure that it did not happen again, Mao needed to not only reclaim power, but he would also need to weed out the people who harbored different visions than the ones that he held. Mao would, once again, follow in Stalin's footsteps and seek to completely eliminate any leaders of the opposition, even those who were close to him, to ensure his legacy.

In May 1966, Mao and his closest allies issued the "May 16 notification" to lay out the problems that they saw with the current trajectory of China. They said that enemies of China had infiltrated the leadership and that they wanted to "create a dictatorship of the bourgeoisie." This was the beginning of Mao instigating a rebellion against the current leaders. It would serve as a springboard for the rise of the Red Guards and the Cultural Revolution. Ultimately, Mao wanted to purge the men who he felt had betrayed him, a feat that would not be simple, considering that the leadership of China had undone much of the damage from the disastrous Great Leap Forward. It would not be easy to change the country's direction, so it was important to turn people against the two leaders who were currently in charge, Liu and Deng.

To accomplish this, Mao started a media campaign to show that even though he was in his 70s, he was still energetic and able to lead China to a better future. The media showed him "swimming" in the Chang Jiang (Yangtze River). Images from the events show him floating on his back more than swimming, though. This was done in preparation of the Cultural Revolution that he wanted to initiate that year.

It was during August of 1966 that Mao finally initiated the revolution, calling on the newly formed Red Guards to challenge the established Chinese politicians. He said that the youth of the day needed to step up to confront China's leaders for forwarding the bourgeoise agenda over the people. Mao also claimed that the leaders lacked the zeal and strength to enact the real changes that would benefit the people.

Removal of Liu Shaoqi and Deng Xiaoping

Liu Shaoqi had been one of the primary leaders following the Great Leap Forward, and he had been considered as Mao's successor. He was the son of a wealthy peasant family and joined the Communist Party of China in the early 1920s. His life was very similar to Mao's, but by 1966, it was clear to Mao that Liu did not have the same values or vision.

Deng Xiaoping had been born into a family in the Sichuan province. Unlike Mao and Liu, Deng's family were landlords, and so, his education was significantly different. When he was sixteen, he was sent to France to study as a part of a student-exchange program. His skills were in managing the military, including as a leader in the People's Liberation Army.

When it became evident that these two men had successfully restored China to a more stable economic position, Mao had reason to fear that his legacy would be considered a bad one. Instead of seeing their success as a positive outcome for China, Mao decided that it was a sign that his legacy was being undone.

So, in retaliation, Mao used the Red Guards to ostracize and undermine both Liu and Deng. Liu tried to prove his dedication to Mao's vision, often attending meetings held by Mao, as being present would demonstrate that he was not acting against Mao or behind his back. Instead of appearing to be working in solidarity with Mao's rising popularity, Liu made himself an easier target of criticism in front of Mao's most rabid supporters. When he tried to criticize himself in October of 1966, it was too late. Mao had been actively demonizing Liu for months at this point, which caused the self-criticism to be seen as an admission of guilt. A month later, Liu was labeled as the "Supreme leader of a black gang," meaning he was an enemy of the people. The first obvious move to remove Liu from power was in 1967 when he and his wife were put under house arrest. Stuck in Beijing, it was only a matter of time before Mao would finally enact his revenge for being sidelined. By the beginning of the next year, he was called "China's Khrushchev," and he was removed from power. By the end of 1968, Liu had no power whatsoever, and he was finally denounced as a traitor to the CPC. Whatever power he had was stripped away, and Liu was kicked out of the party. Imprisoned as an enemy of the people in Kaifeng, Liu would be beaten regularly as an example, partly to show other leaders what would happen if they gained too much control. Mao had once trusted Liu, even appointing him as the next leader, so it was important to show that no one's position was certain if Mao was dissatisfied. After being denied medicine to treat his diabetes, Liu died in 1969. Some say that his death was no accident, as the guards refused to provide him with the diabetes medication that he needed.

As a member of the Red Guards, Deng was treated differently than Liu. He was gradually stripped of all of his standing within the military until he no longer had any power, meaning his decline in power was more gradual. Deng had a loyal following in the military after his illustrious career. To help keep him in check, Mao began to target Deng's son to control the leader better. In 1973, Deng was put through a rehabilitation program based on a recommendation by Mao. Over three years, Deng attempted to ascend in the military ranks, consolidating power as he did so. Following the events at Tiananmen Square in April 1976, the CPC blamed Deng, and he was removed from the CPC. Still, he had a sizable power base, which ensured he did not suffer the same fate as Liu. When Mao died in September 1976, Deng gradually became the de facto leader of the People's Republic of China. Just as he had helped to clean up the mistakes Mao had made in the Great Leap Forward, Deng would again be instrumental in undoing the damage Mao had caused during the decade of the Cultural Revolution.

The Gang of Four

Mao was the leader of the Cultural Revolution, but he was not able to initiate it without the staunch support of other powerful members in the party. Four primary figures aided Mao as he returned to his former position as the primary leader of the nation:

- Jiang Qing, Mao's fourth wife and the leader of the gang

- Wang Hongwen, a Chinese labor activist

- Yao Wenyuan, a Chinese literary critic and politician

- Zhang Chunqiao, a well-known Chinese political theorist

As Mao and the Gang of Four did not act in a way that was transparent, it is difficult to determine which policies and laws implemented during the Cultural Revolution came from Mao directly and which were decided by the Gang of Four.

All four members were devoted to Mao because he had elevated them from lower positions. Before the start of the Cultural Revolution, each member of the Gang of Four held low or middle ranks within the government. Without Mao's elevation of them, they would likely not have attained the power they came to hold. Thus, this made them very loyal to the ideas and decisions of Mao, although they were at odds with each other at times, particularly in the case of Jiang Qing.

Chapter 6 – The Red Guards

The May Fourth Movement of 1919 had left an impression on young Mao. When he began to reclaim his diminished power in the 1960s, he knew that the young people of China were the best way to gain a loyal, fervent base. The fact that the youth of China were more malleable than established leaders was likely another draw for the aging Mao.

To get the youth engaged behind backing him, Mao helped to found the Red Guards. The purpose of this new organization was to provide a place for young people to feel like they had a voice. However, it was also a way for Mao and his loyal followers to control the narrative and to influence the thought processes of future generations.

The Start of the Red Guards

Following the speeches and actions of Mao, students began to band together. Inspired by his vision of a communist utopia, they began to act out against those they perceived as capitalist sympathizers. During the summer of 1966, youths, who ranged from children of elementary school age to young college students, began seeking out oppressors and those who showed either sympathy for capitalism or those who exploited the lower classes.

Mao encouraged suspicion against what was called the Five Black Categories:

- Bad elements

- Counter-revolutionaries

- Landlords

- Rich peasants

- Rightists

Mao also added reactionary academics to the list of people who should be treated with suspicion. This empowered the students and essentially made the teachers in China a target of those they were meant to instruct. No criteria were established for what kind of behavior should be considered suspect, making it entirely too easy to abuse the intentions behind the movement. Students suddenly held a lot of power and could turn on teachers for no reason other than an intense dislike or being given enough bad grades.

Mao and his followers targeted students as a part of their revolution for two primary reasons. First, they were impressionable. Second, it was thought that those who were against Mao and his vision would attempt to influence the youth if he didn't. Essentially, Mao and the other communist leaders were looking to short-circuit any attempt by those who did not agree with their views. So instead of letting them indoctrinate the youth, Mao would, turning the children and young adults of China against anyone who disagreed with Mao's ideology. He was working to harness, or perhaps recreate, a similar spirit that led to the rise of communism in his own youth by using the most impressionable people. If he could inspire the same sense of revolution, he would have the control that he lost following the Great Leap Forward.

One example of the Red Guard fervor was seen at the No. 8 High School in Beijing. One of the leaders of the Red Guards at the school was named Chen Xiaolu, the son of one of the communist revolutionary ministers, Chen Yi. In his apology that he gave in 2013, Chen recalled what occurred at his school. Admitting to his own actions, he stated, "On August 19, I organized a meeting to criticize the leaders of the Beijing education system. A rather serious armed struggle broke out. At the end, some students rushed onstage and used leather belts to whip some of the education officials, including the party secretary of my school." This recollection of the events of that day was just one of many that showed how quickly things turned violent. Despite his aversion to violence, Chen had quickly lost the ability to control the students, as they became overzealous and acted out against the perceived threats. At the end of the event, the vice secretary was crippled, and the secretary would eventually commit suicide after being imprisoned in a storeroom and beaten for two weeks. And this wasn't the only school that had issues with students rebelling. Another school, the Beijing No. 4 High School for Girls, also had students forming Red Guard groups. In August, two teachers were beaten to death by the Red Guards, and another committed suicide.

Both of these events occurred around the time that Mao and Lin Biao, who had become the second chairman of the CPC at the beginning of the month, met with the Red Guards at Tiananmen Square, which took place on August 18th. Mao, as well as Lin, actively encouraged their violent tendencies, endorsing the use of hand-to-hand fighting, as well as the use of blunt objects against any perceived threats to his utopia.

Not all of the persecution was violent, though. Students would sometimes force their teachers to stand in front of classes and assemblies to admit their faults and mistakes, which turned the teachings and ideology of Confucius on its head. Where Confucius' teachings held educators in high esteem, Mao was openly advocating that students hold a higher position themselves. Thus, teachers and educators were subject to the whims and ideologies of their less understanding students. Usually, these demonstrations against teachers were humiliating but not violent. Some would go on to commit suicide because of the shame brought on them and their families.

The Red Terror – The Red Guards Spread across the City

The Red Guards initiated violence nearly from its formation in early June. However, the acts against teachers and authority figures would only escalate over time. In the beginning, the local party leaders did not think that it was necessary to intervene. According to Andrew Walder, an American political sociologist specializing in the study of Chinese society, Mao felt the atrocious behavior was justified to purge the impure elements, viewing "it as a necessary feature of rebellion, and the suffering of victims as acceptable collateral damage." Mao's own words would instigate far worse problems, as students began to feel empowered, even in control.

Mao's wife, Jiang Qing, openly condoned the violence on July 28th, 1966. Speaking as one of the leading figures for the Central Cultural Revolution Group, an organization formed in 1966 to further the ideals and will of Mao, she addressed a rally of students. During her speech, Jiang let them know that the government would not intervene on behalf of the educators, further showing support for whatever the students decided to do, even if it meant violence. Andrew Walder, in his book, *Fractured Rebellions: The Beijing Red Guard Movement*, provides a translation of her words from the event.

> If good people beat bad people, it serves them right; if bad people beat good people, the good people achieve glory; if good people beat good people, it is a misunderstanding: without beatings, you do not get acquainted and then no longer need to beat them.

The actions of the Red Guards came to be known as the "Red Terror," reminiscent of the title given to the events during the French Revolution about 150 years earlier, the Reign of Terror. Nor would it be contained just within the education system. Mao's Minister of Public Security, Xie Fuzhi, would spread the violent ideology to the police and security forces as well. They were instructed during an internal meeting that they were to provide assistance and support to the Red Guards. They were also allowed to enter homes, initiate beatings, and deport anyone who was "found" to be an enemy. The official word was given on August 22nd that the police were not to act against the student movements, which meant that anyone the students identified as enemies were at the complete mercy of those students. Police and security forces were not allowed to provide any assistance to those being persecuted, beaten, or killed.

The result was that between August 1966 and the year's end, the Red Terror allowed for mobs of Red Guards to roam the streets unchecked. Families were evicted from their homes, their possessions taken, and they were forced to leave the city. The confiscation of anything that was considered bourgeois saw millions of dollars' worth of art, currency, and culture stolen from Chinese citizens.

The Red Terror had begun in Beijing, but Red Guards were shipped to other major Chinese cities. From the beginning of August 1966 until the end of September, an estimated 1,772 people were killed in Beijing alone. The Red Guards killed another 534 people in Shanghai and forced more than 700 to commit suicide (some in front of Red Guards, others in private after they were publicly humiliated and beaten). By the end of 1966, it is estimated that more than

100,000 people had been killed as a direct result of the Red Guards' fervor and unchecked power.

Expansion of the Red Guards

Over time, the Red Guards began to include young workers and lower-class people, including peasants. Some were likely swayed by the ideology the Red Guards espoused, but it is likely that many saw a chance at changing their status and situation. Violence became a widespread problem in China, as more people resorted to it as a way of removing the people in power. Like many revolutions before it, such as the French Revolution and the Bolshevik Revolution in Russia, the violence became nearly impossible to contain, and as a result, many innocent people were persecuted and killed.

For instance, people in once revered positions were persecuted for their knowledge. This included monks and landowners, two classes that had always enjoyed respect and more privileges than others. However, this now made them suspect in the eyes of some, while others saw it as an opportunity to remove competition. Public humiliations quickly turned violent. Some people were killed during these attacks, while others would eventually commit suicide because of the humiliation and pain they were subjected to.

It should also be noted that following the rise of the Red Guards, numerous relics and ancient texts were lost. As the number of members of the Red Guards increased, they became more and more destructive. Entire Buddhist temples were decimated, as they sought to destroy anything that could be considered a part of the world of their enemies. Religion was considered wrong, as was anything that was related to the old imperial world. Even the dog breed of the Pekingese began to be slaughtered because of its association with the old world that had been run by the emperor.

The majority of people who died did so at the hands of the Red Guards during the Red Terror. It is unknown exactly how many died as there are no known records. It is difficult to attribute all of the deaths since not all of the victims died immediately.

Ultimately, this persecution ended up stymying education and intellectual growth. Over time, it also caused a slump in the economy that would once again devastate the nation.

Chapter 7 – July 20ᵗʰ Incident

Known as the July 20ᵗʰ Incident in China and the Wuhan incident in the West, the events of July 20ᵗʰ, 1967, showed just how divisive the Red Guard had become. The split between radicals and conservatives reflected divisions within the People's Liberation Army, as well as the government and military.

Before the Red Guards were largely dispersed, their terror moved well beyond the confines of cities and into the rural areas. No longer made of just students, the Red Guards in rural areas included many young workers with little education.

In July 1967, the potential problems posed by the Red Guards came to the forefront in the Wuhan province. The fervor of the Red Guards led to an open fight between the leaders and military of the city and the members of the Red Guard. It was only through the intervention of Zhou Enlai that the fighting was finally resolved. Zhou was more moderate and loathed the abuses that occurred during the Red Terror. However, he was an adept politician with considerable sway because he learned early on to keep his criticism of Mao to private discussions with a few close confidants. It was this perspective of compromise for the betterment of all that would finally establish peace after the horrors resulting from the July 20ᵗʰ Incident.

Wuhan (*Source:*
https://i.pinimg.com/originals/6e/db/88/6edb887890b66772c5f0f80aa
0cb74c7.png)

The Downfall of the Wuhan Leaders and the Rise of the Military

In an effort to remove all opposition from the government, government leaders instructed the People's Liberation Army to oversee the formation of committees that would be loyal to Mao and his vision. The People's Liberation Army began to restructure provincial and municipal governments all across China. To those in charge, the most logical choice of people to execute this effort would have been the military. The network between the military leaders and the regional commanders made it easier to issue orders and receive updates on how the effort was going.

In January 1967, the authoritative figures in the Wuhan province were removed. Over the course of February, the military in Wuhan started to rein in radical attempts to destabilize the progress the People's Liberation Army had made. Chen Zaidao was a general in the People's Liberation Army, and he had commanded the Wuhan Military Region since 1954. In this region, he faced the Workers' General Headquarters, the local radical branch of Mao's ideology. This radical organization was acting in a way that was clearly jeopardizing both the economic and social stability of the region. Unfortunately for Chen, his direction to disband the group was in direct opposition to the permission the Red Guards had been given and, by extension, other radical groups. By disbanding the Workers' General Headquarters in March 1967, Chen ensured that the leaders in Beijing would hear of his own efforts to rein in the excesses of the Red Guards and other radical followers. The majority of them would not look upon his actions favorably, with some being more openly hostile. However, he was a well-respected figure, and it would force the leaders in Beijing to finally confront the numerous issues caused by the unchecked violence.

The People Liberation Army's approach was methodical and strategic. They wanted to implement the change in a way that would minimally disrupt the various aspects of life in the municipalities and provinces. This approach stood in stark contrast to the radical method that overthrew officials and left regions ill-equipped to govern themselves. The conservative approach of the People's Liberation Army compared to the radical Red Guard approach resulted in an open battle in Wuhan in July 1967.

The Wrath of the Radicals

Seeing their own power being taken away, the radicals in Wuhan and Beijing began speaking out against the order, calling Chen's move as suppression. During April of that year, an editorial ran that provided information on the "proper treatment of the Young Generals," as leaders of the Red Guards were called. This was a directive, and it began to tie the hands of the People's Liberation Army so they could not stop the abuses of the Red Guards. The only people within the government who were allowed to counteract the radicals were the leaders in Beijing.

Now that they were given the right to run rampant, the radical elements across the nation were emboldened to act in ways that had been unthought of before. Seizing weapons across the country, they significantly reduced the efficiency of the Chinese military. While this was problematic across China itself, it proved to be incredibly detrimental to North Vietnam, as radicals seized weapons and munitions that were being shipped to aid the communist leader Ho Chi Minh.

With many of their avenues restricted, the People's Liberation Army finally acted by giving the conservative organizations of China weapons and munitions. Violence erupted around the country, and the death tolls were significantly increased because of the arming of citizens.

The consequences of these escalating tensions finally exploded in Wuhan. Radicals wanted to repay the military and its leaders for having curbed their power, staging protests to change the direction that the city was taking. They pointed to the "suppression" of the disbanding of the Workers' General Headquarters as a sign that the new government was not an improvement. Jiang Qing further excited them by endorsing their actions.

Unable to act against these protests, Chen sought to discuss the problems with Zhou Enlai and members of the Central Cultural Revolution Group. One of the few accounts of the decisions of this meeting came from Chen, who said that the group had agreed with him. The majority of them felt that it was in the best interest of the region for the radical elements to be stopped. Whether or not this account is accurate, word of their decision reached the radical members in Wuhan before Beijing could officially issue their verdict on the situation.

Feeling that she had been undermined, Jiang decried that Chen had taken advantage of the situation, and to prevent any action from occurring against the radicals, she actively worked to undermine the progress the meeting had yielded.

While Beijing was caught in its own internal struggle, the two sides in Wuhan continued to clash. Chen had been forming a group called the Million Heroes, which was filled with men who wanted to maintain the status quo and included veterans and other military personnel since the disbanding of the Workers' General Headquarters. Chen said that the group did not take a side between the radical and conservative wings; instead, they sought only to keep order in the region. Clearly, many people on both sides had little reason to believe this claim, as Chen and the group had been actively working to stop radical activities.

In an effort to finally deescalate the rising tensions, meetings were held in the middle of July. Unlike the previous meeting, these meetings were held in Wuhan. Beijing sent several representatives: Zhou Enlai, Li Zuopeng (a member of the 9th Politburo in 1969 and close ally of Lin Biao), Yang Chengwu (a general in the People's Liberation Army and the Acting Chief of General Staff at the beginning of the Cultural Revolution), Wang Li (the man who drafted the "May 16 notification" and the head of party propaganda), and Xie Fuzhi (a military commander who initially backed the Million Heroes but was entirely loyal to Mao and his decisions). Mao even attended a few meetings. This time, though, Zhou took the side of the radicals. He and Mao said that the disbanding of the Workers' General Headquarters had been wrong and that it should be reinstated. However, at the same time, Mao claimed that he was not attempting to unseat Chen.

Xie and Wang remained in Wuhan to carry out the decisions from these meetings, while the rest of the members returned to Beijing. These two party members firmly sided against Chen, and as a result, they made the decision to issue a repudiation of the region's military commanders, particularly Chen Xiaolu, for their refusal to follow orders. The meeting was presented as a further endorsement of the radicals by Beijing.

The Million Heroes were outraged by this portrayal of their attempt to keep order. So, on July 20th, they stormed the hotel where the two men were staying and took them prisoner. Wang Li was detained, and according to some accounts, he was beaten. Despite his position as the minister of public security, Xie Fuzhi was also humiliated. A large group of supporters of the Million Heroes (some reports saying several hundred thousand people) began a march through the city, where they openly criticized the Central Cultural Revolution Group that had backed the Workers' General Headquarters. Eventually, Wang Li and Xie Fuzhi were rescued and brought back to Beijing on July 25th. In all, about one thousand people were killed during the incident. Chen was dragged to Beijing, where he was placed on trial and stripped of his position, which angered many of the officers of the People's Liberation Army.

Although Chen was removed as the commander, he suffered little other punishment. It is likely that Zhou Enlai and Mao Zedong intervened on his behalf since Lin Biao and Jiang Qing were openly hostile to him. However, in Chen's defense, he had actively worked to keep order in a region that was clearly in turmoil.

Other incidents around China certainly put a spotlight on the chaos that the radical wing was sowing across the nation. The division between the radicals and the conservatives would continue for another year. However, the July 20th Incident would force the leaders in Beijing to face the chaos of the Red Guards. By turning on the military, they were significantly weakening their own standing across the globe, which was not what Mao wanted. They would begin to rein in the radical wing, and a year later, they would initiate the Down to the Countryside Movement to curb the chaos inspired by the Red Guard.

Down to the Countryside and the Rise of the Military

By the end of 1968, it was clear that there were too few controls against the violence of the Red Guards. Fearing that the economic downturn would worsen (as it had during the Great Leap Forward), they initiated a new policy called the Up to the Mountains and Down to the Countryside Movement, better known simply as the Down to the Countryside Movement. In truth, it was meant to reeducate the students and workers who had stopped listening to them.

During this movement, which occurred two years after the Cultural Revolution began, members of the Red Guard were sent to learn about the countryside. They were meant to work in the fields and learn about the life of the peasants. Perhaps Mao and his followers were hoping that the violence and destruction would wane as the youths worked in the fields. According to Mao, the government wanted the young people to understand where the majority of the CPC leaders had started. However, their actual goal was to disperse the youth so that they did not continue to destroy so much of the nation's cultural heritage. Ultimately, they were successful, as the violence and chaos that the Red Guard sowed would be stemmed by the youth being sent to work in the fields. It is perhaps ironic that they were forced to learn in a way that was much harsher than school had been, but they would not be allowed to rebel against the much greater abuses that could happen as farmhands.

The things that were lost at the hands of the zealous Red Guards cannot be restored. The party leaders had not fully understood the ramifications of trying to mobilize the youth, so they had no controls in place to prevent their destruction. The errors that were made by the Red Guards were actually similar to several instances of destruction from earlier periods of Chinese history. From 246 to 210 BCE, Qin Shi Huang (which literally translates to "First Emperor of Qin") tried to remove all traces of previous rulers, as he desired to create a history where he was the first ruler. Not only did he destroy physical evidence, but he also had all of the scholars of his time buried alive so that they could not teach any of his predecessors.

Chapter 8 – Border Clashes with the Communist Soviets

As the Red Guards destabilized China from the inside, the Soviet Union saw another opportunity to try to take back lands that the two countries had each claimed at one point or another since the two countries were ruled by a tsar and an emperor. By this point, Mao had managed to do more than just isolate China from the West; he had also isolated China from the nation that had once been his biggest supporter. This meant that China stood alone, which made them appear weak as the internal strife within the country escalated.

The end result of the clashes over these regions was a global realignment. Even as Mao sought to crush all opposition in his country, he began to form alliances with Western capitalist countries. People remember the tension built between the US and the USSR, as well as the tension between the US and China, but the closest the world came to nuclear war was because of the border disputes between China and the Soviet Union.

Sino-Soviet Disputed Borders

(*Source:*
*https://upload.wikimedia.org/wikipedia/commons/thumb/1/11/China_*
USSR_E_88.jpg/270px-China_USSR_E_88.jpg)

Building Tension along the Border

By the 1960s, the relationship between Russia and China had only intensified the tensions about which country had control over the lands on their borders. China felt that the Soviet Union had gained these lands through underhanded treaties, while the leaders of the Soviet Union felt that the treaties were legitimate and should be honored. During 1963 and 1964, the Chinese government started to openly challenge their former communist ally for those areas. Since both countries were nuclear powers, it further intensified the potential dangers both countries posed.

Between 1965 and 1969, the Soviets had been sending forces to the disputed regions. Along the border with China, the Soviet forces

- Ideology over routine

- Practical thought over book-learning

The ideals that Lin had put forward as part of his program were a succinct expression of the ideology of the Cultural Revolution. At the time, Mao had taken a greater interest in the ideas of self-sacrifice and becoming self-sufficient, both of which became valuable following the serious issues caused by the Great Leap Forward. Seeing how Mao's interests and vision were changing, Lin had adapted to further push his agenda.

Lin aided in building the cult of personality that ensured Mao would return to power and retain it. To do that, Lin ensured that the military developed a type of reverence for Mao, sending them to a school that followed Mao Zedong Thought, also known as Maoism. He decided to collect quotes and ideas that Mao had expressed over the years and had them compiled into the *Little Red Book.*

This book was distributed among the military and the Red Guards. To this day, the book is second only to the Bible in the number of books published in the world. Condensed versions were published so that it could be carried in a person's shirt pocket. Men often kept it next to their hearts to show their patriotism and dedication to Mao's ideologies.

In addition to providing a lot of support for Mao, Lin worked with Jiang Qing, Mao's fourth wife, to build her own support base. As she sought to gain power within her husband's government, Lin brought her supporters that could boost her abilities, resulting in the Gang of Four.

All of his efforts to push Mao's agenda and support those closest to him seemed to pay off at the 9th National Party Congress of the CPC held in April 1969. During the Congress, Mao named Lin as his successor. At the same time, the military gained an even tighter grip over the nation as the leaders attempted to exert more control following the chaos caused by the Red Guards. Since the military personnel began to play a larger role in the government, Lin gained more support within the government, as well as from the military.

Lin's power became even more potentially threatening because of the clashes with the Soviet Union during 1969. As a result of these clashes, martial law was declared. Following the declaration, Lin began to remove people who were in opposition to his policies and, perhaps more importantly, those men who threatened his own position as the successor.

Suspicion and Ousting

Despite the relationship that the two men had developed over the decades, Mao was acutely aware of Lin's actions. As Lin began to consolidate his power and remove his opposition, Mao became suspicious of Lin's intentions. The moves that Lin made following the declaration of succession seemed to be a move that would eventually displace Mao. Mao's experiences had taught him to be wary of those who sought power, and fearing that he would again be replaced, Mao began to undermine Lin. Zhou Enlai was eager to align with Mao and push Lin out of his position. It is also possible that Mao's wife joined in the effort to remove Lin, but Chen Boda, Mao's assistant, did not agree that Lin was a threat. He worked to support Lin in the hopes that the CPC leader would not be removed.

Chen would prove to be the perfect warning to Lin. Because of his support for Lin, Chen was removed from public positions and disappeared from public view entirely during the summer of 1970.

Word began to spread that Lin and those who supported him were planning to instigate a coup against Mao. Whether or not this was true, Mao moved against Lin. It is said that while Lin was attempting to flee from Mao, as well as from the fallout of his alleged coup, he was killed in a plane crash in 1971, along with several members of his family. He was immediately vilified by the Gang of Four, whom he had brought together in the first place. By 1974, they had begun an intense campaign to smear his memory.

Like the people whom Stalin had persecuted out of paranoia, Mao and his supporters all but wiped Lin Biao from the history books. However, photographs were not modified to remove him, something that Stalin had done to those whom he removed from power or had executed. Over the years, Lin has begun to be reinserted into the history of the rise of the CPC. He had been instrumental in many of the party's victories, had led the People's Liberation Army, and had provided invaluable services to Mao, particularly *The Little Red*

Book. The introduction of Lin back into history is just another example of how Mao's policies have been undone since his death.

A more immediate problem for Mao and those close to him, though, was the fact that they had already seriously harmed the military with their directions to the military and security not to stop the Red Guards. By binding the military's hands, Mao and his followers created a different set of problems, particularly after the Wuhan Incident. The loyalty that Mao had inspired in the early days was partly lost as he was undermining the rise of military personnel. Instead of giving them power, power was given to youths who went entirely unchecked for more than a year. With the ostracization of Lin and the engaging of activities that had resulted in his death, Mao and his followers had further split the party. Mao did not live to see how the military turned against him, but by the time he died, he had made a number of enemies among some powerful and well-respected members of the military. Without Mao, those who were closest to the late leader would feel the wrath of the military who had become disillusioned by the Cultural Revolution.

Chapter 10 – Health Issues and Slipping Grip on the Revolution

As a part of the cult of personality that Mao had built around himself, physical strength and ability was an important part. The media coverage of his swimming in the Chang Jiang (Yangtze River) is only one example of how he demonstrated that he was still a capable leader. However, he was in his 70s when he built the cult around him. During the 1970s, Mao entered his 80s, and his health was not nearly as robust as the way he had it portrayed it to China.

Deteriorating Health

The displays of his physical fitness were necessary to convince the people that he was capable of leading the nation. This was more of a challenge than one might think, especially considering the life expectancy in China in 1960 was just under 44 years old. Mao was already well beyond that expectancy and had lived through some very difficult years.

To ensure that his image was as a fit, healthy man in his 70s, Mao made sure that no information on his health issues was published. Age was not his only concern; he could not afford to show any weaknesses that could be exploited. As he aged, and as his health deteriorated, Mao had reason to be concerned about how his condition would be perceived, both by the people of China and those who wanted to displace him.

Some of his habits would be considered unhygienic by Western standards. Instead of bathing, he wiped his body down with a warm towel regularly. He was also a heavy smoker, which harmed his lungs, mouth, and reduced his ability to exercise. Instead of brushing his teeth, he used tea to rinse his mouth. Combined with his refusal to see a dentist and smoking regularly, Mao suffered from chronic dental issues, including losing his top row of teeth. He was said to have had problems with body lice as well, which could have been due to the bed that he slept in nearly everywhere he went. Because of the fatty foods that he ate and his unhealthy hygiene, a pustule formed on his chest in 1963. This became a life-threatening abscess because of how poorly he tended to his basic needs.

Even though Mao expressed anger and resentment over the Chinese emperors who had ruled the nation for centuries, he actually lived a life that mirrored their decadence and excess. He not only over-indulged in fatty foods, but he also had four wives throughout his life. Following the belief extolled by the Chinese emperors, Mao likewise kept many mistresses. With his wives, he fathered nine children, and it is unknown how many illegitimate children he had. By 1955, Mao had already suffered from a number of venereal diseases, some of which would never fully disappear. The number of ailments that he suffered as a young man would further weaken him and make regular activities more difficult.

His first known illness occurred in 1924 during the squabbles within the fledgling CPC. The high levels of stress during this period affected Mao, causing him issues like insomnia. The period of political turmoil and the psychosomatic ailments that it caused Mao would continue to impact his health for the rest of his life. When Mao would become stressed, health issues would present themselves, although the symptoms would vary. Sometimes Mao would suffer from constipation and dizziness; other times he would become impotent or depressed. Because of these unpredictable symptoms and how they affected his temper and sleep schedule, Mao expected those around him to keep a more erratic schedule based on when he was active. He would call meetings after midnight and require that all necessary people attend. Mao took medication for his insomnia so he could get some kind of sleep. Over time, though, he developed an intolerance, and he had to take stronger drugs, including barbiturates. Sadly, Mao developed a dependence on these drugs.

His habitual smoking exacerbated illnesses that Mao had as a child. Mao had not been the healthiest youth, and he suffered from regular colds and bronchitis. After suffering health problems for most of his life, Mao finally agreed to allow medical experts to conduct a radiological examination in 1970. They found that he was suffering from pneumonia. When he came down with a more severe respiratory infection a year later, Mao initially refused treatment. It was only after his situation worsened and Mao began to pass out that he allowed specialists to give him a thorough examination. What the medical specialists found was that he was suffering from congestive cardiac failure and emphysema. This led to him finally giving up smoking in 1973.

Slipping Control over the Party

It might seem odd to go on a sidenote about Mao's health, but it played an important role in the decline of Mao's hold over the government and the CPC, as well as what happened after Lin Biao died. His erratic schedule, unhealthy lifestyle, and chronic health problems significantly hindered Mao's abilities as a leader. Knowing that his poor health and old age made him a target for people who sought to replace him, Mao fell victim to a common problem for almost every tyrant—he developed severe paranoia. The most obvious example of his paranoia was in the way he treated Lin Biao nearly as soon as Lin was named his successor.

The last four years of Mao's life were a downward spiral of his slipping power and paranoia. In turn, he became less personable and more irritable. The worse his mental state became, the more the issues manifested as physical problems. His ability to speak was affected, which made him even more irritable, and his physical activities were limited by his weakening muscles and a progressive loss of hearing and sight. After agreeing to limited cataract surgery in 1975, some of Mao's vision was restored.

These apparent weaknesses and Mao's growing paranoia did not go unnoticed by those around him. After Lin's death, many of the leaders began to hope for a change in the nation. By going after the military support of Lin, Mao's popularity decreased, and his biggest supporters began to make power grabs under him.

It was Zhou Enlai who offered Mao the best support after Lin's death. Understanding the situation better than Mao, Zhou helped to keep the fallout from Lin's death from spiraling out of control. Having spent much of his life dedicated to Mao, Zhou had many personal reasons for protecting the chairman. It was Zhou who began to spread the word of Lin's planned coup and smear the late leader's reputation. The CPC, under the direction of Zhou, took control over the military men who had served under Lin. Once these measures were in place, making sure that there were few (if any) people who would extoll Lin's life, the CPC let the nation know of Lin's demise. It was largely Zhou's efforts that ensured that Mao's leadership remained intact after the death of his successor.

As a result of his work to minimize the damage to the party after Lin's death, Zhou had managed to gain more attention among the other leaders, and so, he began to act against some of the persecution that had been perpetuated since the beginning of the Cultural Revolution. He published an article about the role of established bureaucrats, saying they were valuable and should be listened to instead of being persecuted.

However, Zhou's actions were against what the Gang of Four was attempting to do. They began to exclude him from their meetings and tried to further their own agenda instead. Mao was aware of how his supporters were fighting, and he did not approve of the way that the Gang of Four was trying to forward their own agenda. While he did criticize Jiang Qing and the Gang of Four for their excess, he once again failed to check it. As a result, the Gang of Four continued to push their own agenda out to the people.

Mao may not have checked their actions, but he began to look at the Gang of Four, including his wife, with more suspicion. Once, he even went as far as to say that "Jiang is conspiring." As a result, he became more openly critical of the group that claimed to be his most dedicated followers. They were attempting to undermine Zhou's work, even though Zhou ensured that Mao remained in power and that China could find a safe way through the Cultural Revolution.

As a result of the infighting, Mao turned to someone whom he had already persecuted and removed from power once—Deng Xiaoping. By 1975, Mao's health was failing, and Deng had already proved before that he could control the direction of the country. Deng was also not embroiled in the political struggles of Mao's other followers.

This willingness to install someone whom Mao had already removed from power showed just how paranoid and wary he was of his other supporters. Deng was someone that Mao had more control over because Deng was placed in his position solely by Mao. When the national economy began to improve as a direct result of Deng's skills and abilities, Mao was reminded just how different their plans for the future were.

Chapter 11 – The 10th Congress and the Shifting of Power

Between 1975 and 1976, the internal power struggles divided the CPC, and Mao largely let the sides continue their feuding. It is possible that he knew that if they went after each other, they would not be able to attack him. The problem was that this undermined the progress that Zhou Enlai and Deng Xiaoping had made to fix the problems caused by the Cultural Revolution. By the end of 1975, the Gang of Four would finally take the control they felt they deserved.

The 10th National Congress

At the end of August 1973, the leading party members and the government met in Beijing for the 10th National Congress of the Communist Party of China. Zhou had been working to fix the problems of the Cultural Revolution, and as such, one of the primary purposes of the 10th Congress was to hear his report on how his efforts had been going.

Zhou provided a detailed report on the alleged conspiracy of Lin, which made criticism of Lin now a primary focus of the event. The rules of the party were being reformed as a response to the events following Lin's removal and death, though most of the changes were minor. One of the largest changes was the election of members to the 10th Central Committee of the CPC. Some of the new members included the Gang of Four. Although the 10th National Congress accomplished some things, it essentially ensured the continuation of the Cultural Revolution, as it failed to directly address the problems that it had caused.

In January 1974, Jiang Qing called a meeting of more than 10,000 party members and members of major organizations. It was to be the start of the Criticize Lin, Criticize Confucius Campaign. It was notable that Zhou was not included in this meeting. Instead of using it as a way to slander him, Qing would proudly declare, "I didn't invite Zhou to this meeting at all," making it known that the Gang of Four was now working to ostracize the man that was working to repair the financial damages China's economy had suffered during the Cultural Revolution.

When Mao learned that the Gang of Four had not only undermined the man he had relied on to help fix issues but had also tried to broadcast their meeting, he stopped them. Seeing these actions as a power play against him, as it was undermining something he had initiated, Mao was openly critical of Qing and the Gang of Four. However, he did not go any further than criticizing their excessive behavior. Their broadcasts were stopped, but the spreading of the movement to discredit and smear Lin Biao was not stopped.

The Gang of Four again drew Mao's attention when they began to try to undermine Zhou. They tried to criticize him and the bureaucrats Zhou had helped to restore to their previous positions. While they had successfully picked up the movement that Zhou had begun against Lin, they were not adept at creating their own movement. Their attempts to criticize Zhou were petty and showed a lack of understanding about how things worked. By picking on trivial things to criticize, the Gang of Four failed to gain much traction with the people. This was when Mao truly started to see them as a threat to himself. Zhou's work was helping to restore Mao's image, while the Gang of Four was trying to tarnish him.

Results of Deng's Policies and His Second Removal

As mentioned before, the Chinese economy suffered over the course of the Cultural Revolution. According to reports, the industrial and agricultural index dropped nearly ten percent between 1966 and 1967, the first year of the revolution. It went down another 4.2% over the course of the next year. These losses did not include the destruction wrought by the Red Guards, only the financial losses stemming from the bad policies and lack of control over the economy. This time, the problems stemmed almost solely from the policies and persecutions by the government; natural disasters did not exacerbate the economic downfall the way it had during the Great Leap Forward. Mao's and the CPC's policies did not destroy the fields as they had a decade earlier, but they also did not encourage economic growth. Instead, they turned on the people who could have helped to move China forward.

Like during the Great Leap Forward, Deng Xiaoping was able to start repairing a lot of the damage from the bad policies. Deng recognized that the only way to start China on a more progressive path was to restore the intellectuals and the educational system, and so, he worked to make them feel more welcome in the country, a country that had been rejecting them for most of the last decade.

In January 1975, the 4th National People's Congress was held. The purpose of this meeting was to put Deng and Zhou at the center of the party. They wanted to begin advancing the nation by implementing new and progressive types of agriculture, industry, defense, and sciences.

Within a year, Deng's efforts were already starting to show. Where the start of the Cultural Revolution had seen a significant drop in productivity and damage to the economy, after Deng's first year leading the CPC, the output in the agriculture and industry index increased by almost twelve percent. Advancements were seen, most notably in the industry and agriculture sectors, and it was in large part because of the support for Deng. Even Mao openly supported him. Between the progressive movement, the industrialization of the nation, and the restoration of veteran bureaucrats, morale began to rise across the country, as people began to see their daily lives begin to improve. Unfortunately, this would not be seen as a positive thing by Mao, who felt Deng was again leading the country in the wrong direction. This marked Deng as a problem, despite the good that his policies and actions brought.

While it was certainly beneficial to the nation, the changes that Deng was enacting went against what the Cultural Revolution was trying to accomplish. The Gang of Four was able to exploit this to some extent, and Mao could not continue to ignore how Deng was restoring the things that Mao had worked to remove. The rising tension because of this diverging of ideas finally clashed in November of 1975. Mao's apprehensions about Deng would be exploited by Mao Yuanxin, his nephew. Mao Zedong did not even bother to verify the rumors that his nephew told him, instead choosing to act against the man who was fixing the problems that Mao and his close followers had caused. Mao instructed that a new movement be initiated, which came to be called "Criticize Deng, Counterattack the Right-Deviationist Reversal-of-Verdicts Trend."

Instructions to undermine Deng were spread within the party during February 1976. The CPC leaders from around the nation were provided with instructions from Mao. These instructions included a criticism of how Deng had lost the important battle against the enemies of China. Word of the criticism spread all over China, effectively ending Deng's ability to make any more progress.

Zhou Enlai's Death

Another significant blow to progress in China came in early January 1976 when Zhou Enlai died. Mao had continued to rely on Zhou, even as he turned against everyone else. His death was also a significant blow to many of the party leaders.

While most of the country grieved, the Gang of Four saw an opportunity. Zhou had successfully blocked them, so following his death, they sought ways to actively undermine Zhou's legacy. They started their attacks on his memory at his funeral.

The Gang of Four actively blocked others from conducting activities that would show their respect for Zhou. They also worked to manipulate the media to hide how much the leader was being mourned. Despite the efforts of the Gang of Four, millions of people gathered to send Zhou off on January 11th, 1976. And their antics to try to hide the number of people who were grieving actually angered a lot of people in the country. The Gang of Four lacked an understanding of what had made Zhou's movement against Lin Biao so successful. Unlike the people that they slandered, the Gang of Four was not made up of intellectuals, and ultimately, their desire for power without any qualifications would catch up to them.

The Tiananmen Incident

Since the Gang of Four prohibited open grieving, people around Beijing spontaneously went to Tiananmen Square at the end of March to grieve Zhou's death. The more people who joined, the more openly critical they became of the Gang of Four. An increasing number of people decided to start openly acting against the Gang of Four, placing wreaths around the square as well as posters. Over time, they started to give speeches in Zhou's honor. This public display grew into open criticism of the Gang of Four in the form of poems and songs. The people were expressing their thoughts on the political situation and singing about how the populace of China felt about the current situation, as well as their admiration for Zhou.

Similar to how they had made petty and feeble attempts to undermine Zhou in 1975, the Gang of Four began to try to sabotage the movement in Tiananmen Square. They tried to get members of the CPC to halt the displays and demanded that the leaders of different regions monitor the people, warning that they could become a serious problem. The Gang of Four even attempted to command the leaders to keep people from going to mourn Zhou at Tiananmen Square.

This was a significant miscalculation on the part of the Gang of Four. The people were not only mourning the loss of one of their great leaders, but they were also angry at the Gang of Four for trying to prevent them from mourning. They had also suffered unnecessary financial hardships and economic problems until Deng's changes, which only added to their resentment.

Knowing that the Gang of Four and others were trying to suppress their emotions, the movement continued to grow, reaching a fervor on April 4th. Hundreds of thousands traveled to Tiananmen Square, completely ignoring the ban on large gatherings. United in their sorrow and anger, the people essentially launched a demonstration against the people who were obviously trying to control their thinking.

Not believing that the people were capable of their own thought, the Gang of Four decided that Deng Xiaoping must have acted against them. Mao's health was failing, but they still sought for him to stop the mourning. They tried to persuade him that the people who were ignoring their prohibition on it were enemies of the Cultural Revolution, and their expressed emotions were supposed to be proof of that.

After things had settled down that evening in Tiananmen Square, the People's Liberation Army had the posters, wreaths, and other displays of respect removed. When the people arrived the next morning to continue their grieving, they were angered by the elimination of their memorials. With emotions running high, a riot began in Tiananmen Square. The large crowd quickly got out of control, setting police vehicles on fire and forcing their way into government buildings.

Unable to allow the riot to continue, police, security forces, and urban militia were deployed by the Gang of Four to force the mourners-turned-rioters to leave. By the next day, forty people had been arrested, and all of the displays of mourning were once again removed. One positive note during this incident was that there were no deaths.

Similar incidents occurred in other cities around China. Zhou Enlai had been a beloved member of the CPC, and the people knew how much work he had done. However, the damage to Deng Xiaoping was final. Having again been tied to unrest in the country, he was forced out of the party yet again.

Chapter 12 – Mass Killings in China and Devastation in Northern China

Over the ten years of the Cultural Revolution, the violence and killings often caused a lot of upheaval throughout China. The activities of the Red Guards were just the start of the problem. After the Red Terror, there were three more massacres that devastated most of the nation. No one was safe, and terror made people mistrust even their own family members.

The financial devastation may not have been as severe as the problems caused by the Great Leap Forward, but the elimination of intellectuals, educators, and educated people would hinder progress for years to come. The industrialization that Mao wanted to make in the nation was not possible with the kinds of changes he made and the paranoia that his policies instilled in the people. Many of them had been forced into work camps in an attempt to reeducate them, often resulting in their deaths. Some managed to flee, but the damage had already been done. The persecution of the people who could have helped establish China as the leader that Mao dreamed of being devastated the nation. Once Mao died, the nation had too few well-educated people to quickly undo the damage the late leader had caused, due to his support of violence and mistrust of people who could think for themselves.

These problems would only be further aggravated by Mao's refusal to accept aid from other countries.

Events of Mass Killing

The Red Terror in 1966 was only the first of four major violent outbursts in China. The threat of violence hung over the people's heads for most of the decade, but there were times of relative quiet (or at least anxious peace), which would eventually be punctured by extreme violence.

All-round Civil War

Mao celebrated his 73rd birthday, which was on December 26th, 1966, by calling for an "All-round civil war" to restore his power. Mao had already made violence an integral part of reclaiming power, but now, it was no longer limited to the Red Guards—he was condoning it all across the country. The People's Liberation Army called for military support to help remove enemies and their sympathizers. Involving the military only helped to ensure that many people would die. Armed conflicts arose all across China, and the military had a large supply of weapons that they were willing to use against the people. Innocent, unarmed civilians were killed for no apparent reason, pogroms were implemented to reeducate "enemies," and people accused of conspiring against the Cultural Revolution were tortured. Investigations against those who were accused spread fear across most of the country.

The number of casualties during this period range from a half-million to a million. According to a document released by the CPC years after the Cultural Revolution had ended, 237,000 were killed and 730,000 people were disabled.

The second major outbreak of mass killings occurred during 1967. It was primarily an extension of the Red Terror, but it was part of a much larger effort to remove Liu Shaoqi and Deng Xiaoping from power and install Mao as the primary leader again. The Red Guards moved well beyond the confines of the major cities, affecting most of the provinces in the country.

New Organs of Power Killings

Once the majority of Mao's opposition was purged from the CPC and the country, Mao sought to construct a new power structure. This new government was intended to begin with revolutionary committees, which would be established throughout China. Every jurisdiction within China was meant to have a committee by the Chinese New Year, February 1968. However, this deadline was missed because of the upheaval caused by the "All-around civil war." Upset that his new governmental organ was not ready to function as he wanted, Mao initiated political campaigns to empower the committees that had been established.

The first campaign was called the "Cleanse the Class Ranks," and it was meant to discover all class enemies within the party. They were primarily focused on finding members of the KMT who had not yet left, but they also condoned the persecution of people who fit into one of the Five Black Categories (see Chapter 6). In the hands of some politicians, the abuses of this campaign were nearly immediate, as they saw this as the perfect opportunity to eliminate their own opponents.

This was the bloodiest of the campaigns, and it was estimated that over half a million people died as people tried to find a way to climb the ranks in the newly formed committees.

During July 1968, Mao and the party realized that the first campaign had not gone as intended. To rein in the violence, they issued two separate public notices that demanded that all armed conflicts must end. To end the conflicts, the provincial militaries were given permission to suppress the rebel factions. Naturally, this was also abused in many places. New massacres were instigated in the name of ending the massacres that had been caused by the first campaign.

The second campaign occurred in January of 1970 and was called One Strike-Three Anti. All of the new organs of Mao's government had been formed, and so, he wanted to consolidate his power. The government provided some justifications for why this campaign should go forward, but the real reason that the campaign happened was to further remove any opposition that had grown over the years. According to documents from the time, 284,800 people were arrested or killed because they were suspected to be spies, traitors, or counterrevolutionaries. A total of 1.87 million people endured persecution during the ten months of terror of this campaign. It is estimated that the number of victims (both those who were imprisoned, tortured, persecuted, or killed and their surviving families) totaled a full eighth of the nation's population.

The final campaign occurred during February of 1971. In an effort to defend the creation and purpose of the new organs of the government, the CPC announced the "Investigation on the May 16 Counterrevolutionary Clique." Armed with an excuse to instigate a new witch-hunt, people again turned against each other in an effort to gain more political power. Expanding beyond just the people in power, those hunting for detractors also looked for people who were opposed to the new government organs. It was the longest campaign of them all, as it was meant to solidify the place of the committees. Starting at the beginning of 1971, it lasted until 1976 when the Cultural Revolution finally ended.

The Great Tangshan Earthquake

The Cultural Revolution did not run into any serious natural disasters like during the Great Leap Forward. However, on July 28ᵗʰ, 1976, an earthquake that measured 7.6 on the seismic magnitude scale struck the region around Tangshan, located in the Hebei province. The immediate death toll has been recorded as being between 242,000 to 700,000 people.

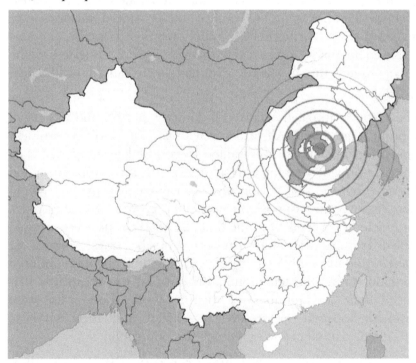

Location of the Tangshan Earthquake

(*Source:*
https://upload.wikimedia.org/wikipedia/commons/3/3d/1976_Tangsh an.png)

Tangshan was one of the industrial cities in China at the time, and an estimated one million people lived there. The earthquake was estimated to have leveled approximately 85% of the buildings. The city had been built on soft soil that was often further softened when the nearby Luan River flooded. When the ground shook, the soil essentially swallowed buildings up. The earthquake was actually so powerful that buildings as far away as Beijing took damage. The distance between Tangshan and Beijing is roughly 87 miles (140 kilometers). The tremors from the quake were felt as far away as Xian, which is 470 miles away (756 kilometers).

In the city of Tangshan, people were trapped under rubble, and coal miners in surrounding areas were crushed by the collapsing mines. Several strong aftershocks further destabilized the region. When the tectonic plates stopped shifting, all of the methods of transportation into the city were destroyed.

Mao's health was so bad during this period of time that he was in the hospital when the earthquake struck. Instead of rushing to help the devastated city, the government instead hurried to check on Mao to make sure that he was comfortable. Word had not yet reached the government in Beijing about the devastation the earthquake had wrecked, but they also did not seem interested in learning what places could have been harmed by the earthquake. It was only when Li Yulin, a coal miner from Tangshan, arrived after a six-hour drive to the capital that they learned what had happened. Even after learning of the devastation from a firsthand account, the government was slow in organizing relief for the city.

For days, the city of Tangshan was forced to struggle through the wreckage without support. They looked for survivors in the rubble and established a place to store the dead in the ravaged streets. The first kind of support that the government sent in was in the form of a plane that released disinfectant over the shattered city in an attempt to prevent the spread of disease.

The People's Liberation Army sent in troops who were ill-equipped to handle any aspect of the problems the city faced. Because the roads and railways to the city had been destroyed, the soldiers had been forced to walk considerable distances just to reach the people in need. They did not have cranes or trucks to move the rubble, so medicine and other necessary emergency equipment were left behind. Tired from having to travel on foot, the soldiers were required to immediately get to work to search for survivors and clean up the wreckage. They didn't even have gloves to begin their efforts. Although they had some limited success, the rescuers were at a serious disadvantage in trying to help the people of Tangshan. With the slow dribble of support, the region suffered significant damage and loss of life before any of the party leaders began to consider how best to address the disaster. It showed how the party had entirely lost focus on bettering China, choosing instead to fight for scraps of power. There were a few leaders who did act, though, and they would gain recognition for their actions and the support of the people following Mao's demise. It is interesting to note that this was in stark contrast to the reactions of Mao's closest supporters.

Hua Guofeng, who became acting premier after the death of Zhou Enlai, realized that the situation was dire. He had been an official in Hunan from 1949 to 1971, near where Mao had grown up. This was likely what attracted Mao's attention, especially since Hua was a staunch supporter. On August 4th, Hua went to visit the city to offer his condolences and support. His apparent interest in the people set him apart from the Gang of Four. Following the disaster, the Gang of Four sent out a broadcast that stated the people needed to maintain focus on denouncing Deng, the enemy, and not be distracted by other matters. According to Jiang Qing, the hundreds of thousands who died were insignificant compared to the millions who would be affected if Deng remained in power.

The government announced the disaster throughout China but hid the devastation from the rest of the world. It would be several years before the world would learn how much damage the earthquake had wrought in the nation. However, the rest of the world was not totally unaware at the time that there had been a disaster, as it was impossible to miss an earthquake of that magnitude. Offers of support and aid were offered to China from many nations, but the Chinese government refused to accept any external aid. Even the efforts of the United Nations to provide assistance were rejected, with the Chinese government telling their people that they should "Resist the Earthquake and Rescue Ourselves."

This lack of regard for the people and obvious concern only for themselves would ultimately be the undoing of the Gang of Four. The earthquake was simply the last straw after a series of careless power grabs that the Gang of Four had made. The devastation from this massive earthquake finally brought about exactly what Mao had feared, though he would not live to see China reject his Cultural Revolution.

Chapter 13 – End of the Cultural Revolution

The end of Mao's life was full of suspicion, paranoia, failing health, and a growing unhappiness with his rule. It was similar to what had occurred following the Great Leap Forward; it had just taken longer to reach that point because he had learned to manipulate the youth in his favor. Without recurring natural disasters to show just how ineffective and disastrous his policies were, it took longer for the people to see the dangers inherent in the fear and anger that Mao had stoked for a decade under the guise of a revolution.

Mao's Death

When US President Richard Nixon visited for the first time in 1972, Mao's health had already significantly deteriorated. Mao extended Nixon another invitation to visit, but Mao would not live to see the second visit.

On September 9th, 1976, Mao Zedong died following a heart attack. The ill will against Mao that had started following the Tiananmen Square incident was quickly quashed following his death, and the people began to view him as a hero once again. The mistake that was the Cultural Revolution was not placed at his feet. Instead, people began to see him as a kind leader who had been given bad advice by those who were supposed to help and support him. All across China, people mourned the loss of a man who had established a strong cult of personality around him.

As others mourned, the Gang of Four focused on trying to eliminate all of their rivals, with their first target being the military and the leaders of the CPC. They attempted to move the capital to Shanghai because they believed it would weaken both the CPC and the government, meaning that they would become essential members of the new government that would form. Mao had jealously guarded the leadership of the country, often undermining those who would follow him. As his staunchest supporters, the Gang of Four hoped to use his death as a way of advancing themselves. The attempt by the Gang of Four to move the capital was met with suspicion by the veteran bureaucrats, the very ones that Zhou Enlai had reinstated. The veterans saw what the Gang of Four was trying to do, and they were prepared to support the government and the CPC that the Gang of Four was attempting to weaken.

The End of the Gang of Four

While the Gang of Four had amassed a considerable amount of power during Mao's reign, once he died, they no longer had a figurehead to follow. Nor did they have someone who would offer them similar protection. Yet, somehow, they failed to realize their own precarious position. Feeling that they were more powerful than other members of the CPC—including Hua Guofeng—they attempted to cement their power over the government, but none of the four succeeded.

Much as Nikita Khrushchev had managed to keep a positive relationship with Stalin long enough to survive the brutal Soviet leader, Mao's chosen successor, Hua Guofeng, managed not to anger or draw suspicion to himself. However, unlike Khrushchev, Hua had actually been chosen by the late leader. This meant that he had a better claim to understanding Mao's vision than the Gang of Four, who had once supported the former leader. Upon Mao's demise, Hua acted quickly to ensure that the power the Gang of Four held was neutralized. This was much easier for him to accomplish because he not only had the support of the government and military, but the people also sided with him. Hua was the one who had showed compassion and a desire to assist the victims of Tangshan. In time, Hua was able to eliminate the Gang of Four by openly denouncing them as the cause for the excesses and problems that were the direct results of the Cultural Revolution. Instead of accusing the man who began the terror and problems for being wrong, although it is likely that Hua would not have done that anyways, Hua shifted the blame to the Gang of Four. They had shown open contempt for the people, making it clear that their interest was in themselves and power, not in leading the nation in a better direction.

On October 6th, 1976, less than a month after the death of Mao, Hua had the former leader's wife, Jiang Qing, arrested. The other members were also rounded up and imprisoned alongside her, their power officially destroyed.

It was during this time that the name Gang of Four emerged. The four had played large roles in the direction of the nation, but they had not been officially identified as coordinating leaders in the same way as the media would tie them together.

The Gang of Four did have a power base in Shanghai, which could have posed a major problem for Hua and his people. By offering those supporters a chance to speak, Hua lured the majority of the people who supported the Gang of Four to Beijing, where they were quickly arrested.

Within a few years, Hua was able to almost completely turn the people against Mao's staunchest supporters. All four were put on trial for treason in 1981. In addition to treason, they were charged with a host of crimes, including causing the death of 34,375 people. To earn greater support, the new government charged the four with aiding and endorsing the persecution of hundreds of thousands of innocent citizens. Wang and Yao confessed, expressing regret at what had happened. Wang Hongwen, who was once thought to be the one chosen to be Mao's successor, was given a life sentence for confessing his crimes, but he was later moved to a hospital in 1986, dying six years later. Yao Wenyuan was given twenty years imprisonment for his role in the Cultural Revolution. He was finally released in 1996 and died nine years later.

Zhang Chunqiao protested that he was innocent of the charges. Jiang Qing, Mao's widow, was the only woman of the group, and she expressed that she had only done what Mao had instructed her to do. Both were given death sentences with a two-year reprieve, though the government never carried them out, instead turning their death sentences into life imprisonment. Zhang was released in 1998 because of a diagnosis of pancreatic cancer, and he died in 2005. Jiang lived under house arrest starting in 1984. Reports say that Mao's widow was diagnosed with throat cancer around 1991. To avoid the pain associated with the disease, she hung herself that same year at the age of 77.

A New Direction

With the arrest of the Gang of Four, the Cultural Revolution was finished. They had been trying to incite more action to further the Cultural Revolution, something that Hua was not interested in prolonging any further. His vision for China was more closely aligned with Zhou and Deng's vision than Mao's.

No longer under the influence of Mao and his supporters, the People's Republic of China began to follow a more progressive path. Hua would establish better relations with Western countries, although he did keep many of the controls in place to ensure that the government retained its influence over the population. Despite this, he still moved the nation's economy toward a more capitalistic model. The mix of a liberated economy and a controlling government is still in place today.

Chapter 14 – Lasting Effects

The number of people who died as a result of the decade-long Cultural Revolution is not certain. With a weakened economy, a fractured CPC and government, and a people who were tired of the years of violence, Hua Guofeng needed to work to restore morale while rebuilding the country. Schools had largely been closed throughout the Cultural Revolution, and the nation had killed or persecuted intellectuals for so long that they were starting to rebuild educational institutions at a severe disadvantage.

The Recent Acknowledgement of Regret and Remorse

In 2014, some members of the Red Guards issued apologies over what had transpired during the Cultural Revolution. They admitted to the persecution, torture, and killing of millions in the name of communism and supporting Mao. Instead of helping to build the utopia that they had envisioned, the Red Guards had helped instill fear and suspicion throughout the country. The openly hostile environment did not help build the world they envisioned; instead, it became a place where no one felt safe.

Even their apology was divisive. Those who suffered under the Red Guards said that after fifty years, their apology was both too little and too insincere to be believed. Others felt that the members issuing the apology were doing so to besmirch the name of Mao, who is still revered in China today. However, it should be noted that those willing to issue an apology must do so in a limited capacity and be cautious about how they issue it. It is easier to find these kinds of apologies from outside of China since many major Chinese stations are not allowed to air them.

Some of the apologies are quite emotional. One senior leader of the Red Guards, Song Binbin, had been responsible for the students in her school. When they turned violent, they ended up beating the vice principal to death.

Victims and relatives of those who were killed are more outspoken against Mao. To them, the apologies are not only too late, but they are also the attempts of those to absolve themselves of what they did. Not all of these victims reject the apologies, and they see a hopeful sign that the wrongs from the Cultural Revolution will finally be acknowledged.

As more people come forward to apologize, it appears that the tragedies and wrongs of the Cultural Revolution may finally be spoken of in more detail. However, these apologies are still very much on a personal level, not on a larger scale. During the 1980s, the Chinese government said that the Cultural Revolution was a mistake but would not further classify or discuss any accountability for what occurred. The fact that apologies are being allowed on some level could indicate that something more will come later. Time will only tell if the apologies evolve into something more or if they will help heal some of the wounds from the events during the decade remembered as the Cultural Revolution.

Conclusion

The Cultural Revolution lasted for a full decade, sending the nation spiraling into a series of violent clashes, as well as economic turmoil. Mao has now been seen as the primary driver of the disaster that resulted in the deaths of many people and saw agricultural ruin. After all, the Cultural Revolution was Mao's way of restoring his image as a true leader and removing the two men who had helped to undo the damage done under Mao's policy of the Great Leap Forward.

Just as problematic for Mao was the way Liu Shaoqi and Deng Xiaoping had started to incorporate more progressive ideas that Mao considered to be dangerous for a communist country. The best way for him to restore his communist vision for the country and to claim the power he felt he should have was to build a cult of personality around himself. Once he had regained the adoration of the people, he was able to act against the two leaders. And from there, he sought to remove all possible detractors, leading to ten years of bloody conflicts.

The Cultural Revolution was more than just a way for him to ensure that his vision would be perpetuated even after death. It was also a way for him to live forever, as it was a way for him to create the communist utopia he dreamed of. Violence was not only encouraged during this revolution but was fully endorsed by Mao and his main followers almost from the beginning. They felt it was necessary in order to achieve the vision Mao desired, and those who died—even the innocent—were simply collateral damage.

The damage wrought to the Chinese people, culture, and economy took decades to rectify. While Mao Zedong was a capable figurehead, he had repeatedly proven that he was not the best man to actually lead the country. His desire to retain his power led to two of the darkest periods in modern Chinese history at the cost of millions of lives.

Part 2: Mao Zedong

A Captivating Guide to the Life of a Chairman of the Communist Party of China, the Cultural Revolution and the Political Theory of Maoism

Introduction

Mao Zedong – was known as "Chairman Mao" to millions of Chinese citizens – is recognized alongside Chiang Kai-Shek and Sun Yat-Sen as one of the most influential figures of modern Chinese history. His political control of the nation waned during his later years, but he remained the Chairman of the Communist Party of China since it was established in 1949 to the day he died (September 9, 1976). As the founding father of the People's Republic of China and the centerpiece of one of the world's most intense personality cults, the extent of his influence is difficult to understate[i].

Mao was not just a communist revolutionary or a political leader. He was also a poet, a political theorist, and a brilliant orator. His similarly influential successor Deng Xiaoping[ii], who served as the de facto leader of the People's Republic of China from 1978 until his retirement in 1989, is acknowledged worldwide for steering the nation towards economic growth. His legacy can be judged by the physical markers of economic development: infrastructure in the form of roads, highways, buildings, factories, skyscrapers, cities, gross domestic output, etc.

While Mao is credited for catalyzing China's transition from a mostly agrarian nation into a modern industrial powerhouse, his legacy cannot be confined to economics alone. Deng's pragmatism and emphasis on individual self-interest may prevail in contemporary China, but Mao still inspires widespread devotion. Some prominent pictures and statues of Mao in the country have been quietly removed, but his portrait still figures prominently in Beijing's Tiananmen Square. He joins the ranks of some of the world's most famous community cult-of-personality leaders in having his corpse being on public display: Russia's Vladimir Lenin, Vietnam's Ho Chi Minh and North Korea's Kim Il Sung and Kim Jong-il. His embalmed corpse lies in a crystal cabinet within a stately Soviet-inspired memorial hall in the middle of Tiananmen Square, attracting long lines of visitors.

His legacy as a political leader is marked by significant successes and catastrophic failures – a historical reality that remains controversial in contemporary China's censor-prone, one-party state. His contributions to the nation as a political genius and ideological visionary – raising its average life expectancy, championing gender equality, improving popular literacy, promoting the collectivization of agriculture, ensuring accessibility to medical services, ushering in a period of unity and stability after decades of civil war and foreign invasion, restoring its sense of pride, dignity and confidence after a "Century of Humiliation" and positioning it towards the world economic and military power it is today – were magnified and glorified during his reign.

His theories, clever military strategies, and political policies (which are collectively known as Maoism) inspired anti-capitalism and anti-imperialist sentiments. Mao's charisma and force of personality gained him widespread approval, respect, admiration, and devotion in his home country. He was also able to charm Western intellectuals and political leaders like the American journalist Robert Snow (who wrote his first biography), Harvard professor John K. Fairbank, feminist philosopher Simone de Beauvoir, and French philosopher Jean-Paul Sartre[iii].

Mao's image as a benevolent protector of the people and his humble origins from the peasant class made it easier to suppress the brutal realities of his authoritarian rule. His grandiose ambitions for China to become a military superpower lead to a disastrous nation-wide diversion from agriculture to industrial arms-making. As a result, an estimated 45 million people starved to death during The Great Famine from 1958 to 1961.

Under his Cultural Revolution (1966 – 1976), Chinese culture and intellectual life suffered tremendously. Chinese classics of literature, poetry, and philosophy were burned across the nation. Foreign works of art, literature, and culture were banned for being "counterrevolutionary." Respected artisans and intellectuals were stripped of their respect, dignity, and professions.

Today, Mao's legacy can inspire slavish devotion, outright condemnation, as well as a hesitance to look too closely at the negative aspects of his legacy. The fact that his influence spanned over nearly three decades also makes it difficult to arrive at a holistic understanding of his impact on China. The official line from the

Community Party of China, which was popularized by Deng Xiaoping, is that Mao was "70 percent correct and 30 percent wrong"[iv]. This biography will detail Mao's remarkable journey, from being the son of a peasant to one of modern history's greatest – and highly polarizing – leaders. It aims to provide a better understanding of Mao as a person and to try to unpack the personality traits and personal experiences that shaped his worldview and actions.

Chapter 1 – Early Life

Mao was not born into political or intellectual privilege, but he was not born into poverty either. He was born on December 26, 1893, in the remote village of Shaoshan in the Hunan province. His father, Mao Yi-chang, was unlike the average Chinese peasant who toiled in poverty. Despite only possessing two years of formal schooling, he had improved his status and wealth through hard work, frugality, and shrewdness'. As a rich grain dealer and land-owning farmer, he expected his son to gain knowledge of the Confucian classics, accounting and bookkeeping, and to contribute to his business when he became older. To him, the pursuit of knowledge was for purely utilitarian ends. Mao would recount one of his father's favorite sayings to his daughter Li Min: "Poverty is not the result of eating too much or spending too much. Poverty comes from an inability to do sums. Whoever can do sums will have enough to live by; whoever cannot will squander even mountains of gold!'"

His father was stern, authoritative, and prone to violent bursts of temper. Despite being the eldest son (he was technically the third-born son, but his two older brothers had died in infancy), Mao was not spared from harsh beatings by his father. His two younger brothers Mao Zemin and Mao Zetan and his adopted younger sister Mao Zejian were also beaten. Mao and his siblings found refuge and comfort in his gentle mother Wen Qimei, who was a devout Buddhist. She tried to share her religious outlook with her son and often brought him to the nearby Buddhist temple to pray. She hoped he might decide to become a monk and would promote peace as he followed in the Buddha's footsteps.

Mao would fulfill neither of his parents' ambitions for him. With his exceptional memory, he easily mastered the Confucian principles that his father had sent him to learn in elementary school. He was nevertheless personally uninspired by Confucius' emphasis on moral perfection and filial piety. Instead of adhering to Confucius' commandment that children obey their parents and elders, Mao openly contradicted and opposed his father and teachers (and strategically used Confucian quotations to support his position). His biographers Jung Chang and her husband John Halliday noted that he would argue that his father, being the older individual, should perform more manual labor than him, a younger child. They point out that this was "an unthinkably insolent argument by Chinese standards," which certainly did not elevate individual conscience over paternal authority.

From a young age, Mao demonstrated an unconventional and highly atypical (given the cultural context) penchant to assert his own will and defy traditional authority. He was also able to use his intelligence to manipulate his adversaries. In their biography, Chang and Halliday describe how his argument with his father (in front of several guests) played out:

"My father scolded me before them, calling me lazy and useless. This infuriated me. I called him names and left the house ... My father ... pursued me, cursing me as well as commanding me to come back. I reached the edge of a pond and threatened to jump in if he came any nearer ... My father backed down [...] Old men like him didn't want to lose their sons. This is their weakness. I attacked at their weak point, and I won!"

When he was 13, he could no longer tolerate his teacher's reliance on physical abuse as a pedagogical tool.   Contented   with   the amount of learning he had amassed thus far, his father happily arranged for him to begin working full-time on the family farm. (He had been assigned various farming tasks by the time he was six years old). However, Mao was not personally interested in his father's commercial pursuits, Confucius' humanism, or his mother's religious outlook as a child.

Instead, he was passionately devoted to Chinese historical literature that described heroic uprisings, upheavals, and revolutions. He ardently consumed narratives of adventurers, warriors, knights, and fighters in texts such as *The Biography of the Ever-Faithful Yue Fei, Water Margin, The Three Kingdoms, Journey to the West* and *The Romance of Sui and Tang.* He kept his reading habit hidden from his father, who would become outraged at the sight of such a "useless" pursuit. When he came across Zhen Guanying's *Words of Warning to an Affluent Age* (1893), he began to develop an interest in the politics of the era. Zheng's book presented a vision of how to modernize China by deserting its traditional Confucian order and establishing a British-type constitutional monarchy.

While Mao was broadening his intellectual horizons, his parents were making plans for his future without his consent. By the time he learned of their plan to marry him (at 14) to Luo Yigu, the daughter of a rural intellectual who was four years older than him, his marriage contract to her had been signed. (Mao Yichang himself had been married at 15). The wedding date had been agreed on, and his father had sent the customary gifts and bride-price to his soon-to-be father-in-law Luo Helou. Mao revealed to his first biographer John Snow that he had not consummated the marriage[viii]. Not long after his wedding, he deserted his parents, family, and wife to live in the house of an unemployed student in Shaoshan. Luo Yigu would quietly endure the humiliation of being described as "neither a married woman nor a maiden" for two years, before dying of dysentery shortly after her twentieth birthday on February 11, 1910[ix].

Free from the demands of his parents and responsibilities on the farm, Mao could focus solely on his reading. During this formative time, he explored nonfiction historical and political texts. He digested older texts like *Records of the Grand Historian* by ancient Chinese historian Sima Qian and Ban Gu's *History of the Former Han Dynasty*. He also read texts that explored China's contemporary struggles with foreign aggressors and invaders, such as Feng Guifen's *Personal Protests from the Study of Jiao Bin* (1861)[x]. After reading a pamphlet written by young Chinese revolutionary Chen Tianhua, he developed an acute understanding of the losses and humiliation that China had suffered at the hands of Japan and Britain.

When Mao eventually reached out to his father to ask for financial assistance to pursue his education when he was 16, he decided to forgive his "ungrateful son." Mao enrolled in Dongshan Higher Primary School, which was located approximately 15 miles away from Shaoshan. There, Mao would be exposed to contemporary subjects such as physics, chemistry, and biology. This was the first time Mao ventured beyond the cloistered confines of his native village.

Mao may have had grand ambitions for himself in his head, but his classmates fixated on his provincial origins. At his new school, Mao's peers were the arrogant sons of wealthy landlords from the neighboring Xiangxiang district. They disapproved of his regional dialect and lack of an impressive wardrobe. Mao made very few friends and suffered under the hostility he received from the majority of his peers.

Instead of keeping a low profile, he was determined to succeed. He endured the insults and eventually impressed his teachers with his intelligence and capacity for hard work. His education provided further exposure to the various rulers that attained glory in China's illustrious past: Yao and Shun, Qin Shi Huangdi, and Wu Di. He also gained exposure to foreign history and developed an admiration for the military and political acumen of Western historical icons like Napoleon, George Washington, Catherine the Great, and Abraham Lincoln[xi].

He was particularly inspired when he learned of Japan's victory over Russia in 1905. The victory was symbolic on two fronts. On the one hand, it was a triumph of an Asian country over an intimidating European power via the embrace of political modernization. On the other, it was a victory of a constitutional monarchy over despotism. The idea of China emerging from the backwaters and pursuing a path to similar eminence on a global scale was within his consciousness as he decided to leave Dongshan School for a middle school in Changsha: the capital city of the Hunan province.

Chapter 2 – Political Awakenings

Changsha was over three thousand years old and had recently been the primary base for the suppression of the Taiping Rebellion[xii]. It opened to foreign trade in 1904. When Mao arrived at his first city in early 1911, he experienced the wonders of cosmopolitanism. Changsha was home to a few Western schools, including a missionary medical college. Mao was awed by the sight of electric lights, stone-paved streets, and the city's towering stone wall. He was most amazed, however, by the sight of the railroad (that had been constructed three years earlier) and the locomotive train. There were a small number of foreigners in the city, mainly the Americans who had established a Yale University branch and a hospital there.

Mao was pleasantly surprised he had gained admission to a vaunted school in the city. Here, he was exposed to new theories and ideas from the West through the works of reformers such as Liang Qichao and Sun Yat-sen[xiii]. One could argue, however, that his "real education" occurred through the six months he spent as a soldier. On October 10, 1911, an anti-monarchical uprising against the Qing dynasty began in Wuchang, the capital of Hubei Province. Many soldiers from the Eighth Engineer Battalion of the New Army there were members of the revolutionary Progressive Society, which were closely linked to the Revolutionary Alliance led by Sun Yat-Sen. They quickly gained control of the entire city and sparked a wave of anti-Manchu uprisings in neighboring cities. Within just two weeks, the rebellion had spread to Changsha. When November ended, fifteen out of China's eighteen provinces had defected from Qing authority.

News of these transformative events galvanized Mao's evolution from a patriotic supporter of the Chinese monarchy to an anti-monarchical revolutionary. Even before he received news of the Wuchang uprising, he had decided to cut off the long pigtail that all Chinese men were required to wear as a sign of submission and loyalty to the Manchus. As the conflict between the revolutionaries and Qing monarchy escalated, Mao decided to join the revolutionary Hunan army as it made plans to invade the north.

On December 25, Sun Yat-Sen returned to China. Instead of negotiating with the prime minister appointed by the Qing court (Yuan Shikai), Sun prepared for a military confrontation. He proclaimed the founding of the Republic of China in Nanjing on January 1, 1912 as the president of the National Assembly (which was composed by delegates from the 15 rebellious provinces)[xiv]. There was to be, however, no major military conflict. Most of the National Assembly delegates wanted the monarchy to be dissolved, but they did not want a revolutionary like Sun Yat-Sen to assume control of the newly-formed republic. After China's last emperor – the six-year-old Pu Yi – abdicated the throne on February 12, 1912, Sun Yat-Sen resigned from his position as Yuan Shikai was elected the provisional president of the Republic of China.

Mao did not experience significant military action during the six months he spent as a soldier. He nevertheless obtained a first-hand experience of military life – a realization of his fascination with the famed military strategists of history. As a soldier, Mao was paid a relatively high salary of seven silver dollars each month. He would reveal to Edgar Snow, however, that he saw himself as a class apart from most of his fellow soldiers, who were illiterate and poor (and thus joined the army for food)[xv]. Instead of carrying water from outside the city like his comrades, he decided to buy it.

After Mao was discharged from the military, he explored his choices. He certainly did not have a clear idea of what he wanted. He first decided to enroll in police school, and then decided to try his hand at soap making. After that, he pursued law school, a commercial middle school, and then a higher commercial public school. In the spring of 1912, he decided to enroll at Hunan Higher Provincial School. Rather than sticking to the prescribed curriculum, however, he pursued independent learning at the Hunan provincial library. There, he studied the classic texts of the Western liberal tradition alongside collections of foreign history, Greek myths, and international geography. At 19, he had his first encounter with a world map. He also gained a foothold in political activity by helping to establish a number of student organizations. This included the New People's Study Society (est. 1917-18). Several members of this society would eventually join the Communist Party.

Angered by his lack of direction and numerous changes of plans, his father compelled him to enroll in a professional program (or else proceed without his financial assistance). Despite his humble origins, Mao considered himself to be an intellectual, i.e. a class above the peasants, coolies, and soldiers who were required to contribute manual labor[xvi]. The revolution may have occurred, but the vast majority of Chinese citizens at the time were still illiterate and working as construction workers, coolies, peddlers, and porters. Unwilling to pursue manual labor or earn his living as a tutor, he decided to heed his father's wishes. In 1913, he enrolled at the Hunan Provincial Fourth Normal School with plans to become a teacher. In March 1914, the local authorities decided to merge the school with the more reputable and larger Provincial First Normal School.

The First Normal School was relatively new, having been founded in 1903 – towards the last years of the Qing dynasty. The people of Changsha referred to it as the "Western palace" because of its European architecture, and the teachers Mao encountered there embodied its structural modernism[xvii]. They had been educated overseas and were well-versed in French, Japanese and English. A few of them would exert a significant influence on the young Mao. Yuan Jiliu taught him to write impressive essays, while Xu Teli and Fang Weixia (who were both members of the Revolutionary Alliance and had participated in the 1911 Revolution) solidified Mao's patriotism and his faith in the idea of China being governed as a republic.

The educator that Mao held in the highest regard was Yang Changji, the head of the school's philosophy department and a devoted fitness enthusiast. Yang had studied in Japan, Germany, and Scotland, and could easily impress his students with his formidable knowledge of both Chinese and Western ethics and philosophy. He also taught logic and pedagogy and subscribed to Western liberalism – which he saw as equivalent to the philosophies of Confucian thinkers Wang Yangming and Wang Chuanshan. Mao recounted his admiration for Yang to his friend: "When I think of [his] greatness, I feel I will never be his equal." He described Yang's impact on his character to Edgar Snow: "He believed in his ethics very strongly and tried to imbue his students with the desire to become just, moral and virtuous men in society." The admiration was mutual. Yang commented that "it is truly difficult to find someone so intelligent and handsome ...many unusual talents have come from peasant families."

Mao thus participated in many of the long hikes that Yang organized as well as the Sunday discussion sessions he held in his home. Yang presented attractive ideas of how liberalism and individualism could be used to create a democratic reimagining of Chinese society. He promoted the concept of strong individual personalities that arose from intense self-cultivation and encouraged his students to achieve self-actualization to help restore the nation's glory. These ideas would prove to be dangerous to Mao's fellow countrymen since they created the perilous logic that morality was relative, and thus could be set aside for the goals of a "strong individual" to pursue his own ends.

His thinking on the relationship between a political leader and the masses can be gleaned from his 1912 essay on Lord Shang Yang[xviii], an ancient Chinese minister whose radical reforms had strengthened the state of Qin. Mao was ready to overlook the cruelties of his dictatorship (which led to a massive death count) on account that he had achieved considerable political power. He lamented the "ignorance" and "stupidity" of the Chinese masses for distrusting and fearing him.

Mao's concept of self-improvement and self-realization was not limited to his intellectual pursuits alone. Together with his classmates, he would pursue rigorous forms of physical and spiritual training as a form of preparation for their future endeavors as the nation's reformers. This included hiking through the fields and mountains, hiking along the city's walls, sun-bathing when the weather was hot, "wind bathing" when spring brought gusts of winds, swimming in the river during winter, and sleeping out in the open when it began to snow. Mao was shaping himself up to be the hero that China needed, ready to undo the humiliations inflicted by foreign powers and the injustices wrought by its long line of corrupt monarchs, court officials, feudal lords, oligarchs, and military leaders.

As Mao explored his dreams of political power and the strategies needed to maintain it, the nation's political situation became increasingly perilous. Yuan Shikai, the general who had been elected as the provisional president of the Republic of China, had died on

June 6, 1916, because of uremia. His death occurred amid tumultuous times. Yuan's attempt to impose an explicitly dictatorial order in the nation had created conflict with Sun Yat-sen's revolutionaries and local military oligarchs. The Revolutionary Alliance (now known as the Guomindang, or Nationalist Alliance) openly opposed his rule and had been outlawed in November 1913, forcing Sun Yat-Sen to flee to Japan. Yuan's decision to appease Japan's demands for Germany's territories in China after World War I began stirring anger and indignation across the nation. Yuan died as civil war consumed the country, and was replaced by General Li Yuanhong. As central power dissolved, provinces across the country – including Hunan, where Mao was – plunged into chaos as local militarists fought for control amongst themselves.

In the fall of 1917, Mao decided the time for contemplation had given way to the time for action. He had been named the best student in his school in June 1917 and was beginning to demonstrate his organizational capacities. He became the leader of the Student Union and helped to restore the evening workers' school that provided classes for unemployed laborers in the city. In November that year, he helped to organize a student volunteer guard (with only bamboo sticks and wooden rifles) that would protect students – especially female ones – from improper behavior from soldiers. Mao even organized a defense against the army's demands to convert the school into a barracks. In April 1918, Mao helped to establish the Xinmin xuehui (Renovation of the People Study Society) to connect with other students who desired to improve the nation. The society aimed to make sense of the new modes of thinking that had appeared across the nation, and to achieve its lofty aim: "To improve the life of the individual and of the whole human race." Each member had to follow five simple rules:

"1. Do not be hypocritical;

2. Do not be lazy;

3. Do not be wasteful;

4. Do not gamble;

5. Do not consort with prostitutes".

Their sense of how to improve the "whole human race" was nevertheless far from defined. The group generally agreed on being anti-imperialist, but otherwise, their ideas flirted inconclusively with Kantianism, Confucianism, liberalism, utopianism, and democratic ideals in their quest to achieve national progress. When Mao graduated from the Normal School in June 1919, he was similarly devoid of a clear sense of what he wanted to do next. Instead of pursuing full-time work, he lived alongside the Xiang River with several friends and spent his time amongst nature.

Chapter 3 – Beijing

A letter from his favorite teacher Yang Changji, who was now working at Peking University, provided an alternative course of action. It detailed an attractive opportunity to study in democratic, revolutionary France – via the Chinese Society for Frugal Study in France, a work-study program that intended to help young Chinese citizens gain access to French education while working to pay for their expenses. The budding intellectuals would work alongside the workers and laborers, bridging the categorical gap between workers and intellectuals and eventually helping to rejuvenate China. Mao and his cadres were excited at the possibility of studying in France and made plans to travel to Beijing to confirm their participation.

Before leaving for Beijing, Mao visited his mother, Wen Qimei. She had been plagued by stomach ulcers for a long time and had recently developed inflammation of her lymph nodes. She had also decided to leave her husband to stay with her older brothers in her home village due to irreconcilable differences. Mao hoped she would travel to Changsha to benefit from medical testing, but she declined. He revealed his plans to visit Beijing without mentioning the possibility of studying in France.

In August 1919, Mao embarked on his first train ride to Beijing (from the neighboring city of Wuhan) with twenty-five of his comrades. There, Yang Changji agreed to accommodate Mao and three of his comrades in his home. Mao had met his teacher's daughter Yang Kaihui before, as a young girl. She was now a young woman, and Mao was awestruck by her beauty. Kaihui had heard her father proclaim Mao's intelligence and accomplishments before and was similarly smitten. Neither party, however, were immediately transparent about their feelings.

After a few days, Mao relocated to a tiny apartment with three rooms with seven of his friends. They did not have enough money for heat, so they huddled close to each other at night for warmth. The apartment was near Peking University and the Forbidden City, providing Mao with easy access to some of the city's architectural and intellectual wonders. Peking University was the center of The New Culture Movement, which involved Chinese intellectuals parsing through various economic, political and social theories that would help to improve the nation. Traditional Confucian ideals were swept aside to make way for democracy, humanism, individualism, and liberalism. Mao was strongly attracted to *New Youth*, the journal of the moment, and the leaders of the movement: Cai Yuanpei, Rector Cai, Li Dazhao, Hu Shi and Chen Duxiu.

In October 1918, Professor Yang Changji secured him a job as an assistant librarian at Peking University. Mao would be working under Li Dazhao, director of the library and an economist, historian and philosopher. Li was one of the first intellectuals to consider how the new tenets of Marxism could be applied to China. Li was also one of China's first intellectuals to turn to the Bolshevik revolution in Russia as a chief source of inspiration. Li would personally familiarize Mao with Marxism and Bolshevik ideology once he began working in the university library. Mao would also be invited to participate in political activities. His intellectual horizons broadened, Mao decided to attend lecturers at Peking University and joined university societies focused on modern literature, journalism, and philosophy.

Despite his position under Li Dazhao, Mao would fall under the ideological spell of Chen Duxiu, the dean of the College of Letters. He would reveal to Edgar Snow that Chen had influenced him "perhaps more than anyone else." Chen did not support Marxism or Bolshevism, believing instead in democracy, humanism and personal freedom. Mao's intellectual allegiance with Li meant he was distanced from Li's support for Bolshevism. He did, however, become personally interested in Peter Kropotkin's anarchism, partly because of the importance it placed on individualism. Mao's exposure to anarchist texts in the library – coupled with the fact that his arrival in Beijing was triggered by a French work-study program organized by anarchists – planted increasingly radical thoughts in his mind.

Unfortunately, his dreams of studying in France were hindered by his relative ineptitude at languages. To be selected for the program, he would have to pass a French language examination. He was also burdened by anxieties about his social status as an assistant librarian from the southern countryside. Mao was brought into the social and intellectual fold by Li Dazhao and Chen Duxiu, but many other established intellectuals at the university ignored him.

As some of his comrades embarked for France, Mao received news that his mother's health had worsened. Instead of departing immediately to her side, however, he made several detours. Before leaving Beijing on March 12, he spent twenty days in Beijing with students who would soon be heading to France. He would arrive in Changsha on April 6 but waited until April 28 to write to his uncles to inform them that he was on his way home to Shaoshan. Wen Qimei would die on October 5, 1919, without seeing her son for the last time. Mao nevertheless arrived in time for her funeral and recited a poem he had written himself. When his father died less than four months later, Mao did not travel back home to attend his funeral[xix].

Chapter 4 – May Fourth and the New Culture Movement

Mao did not return immediately to Beijing after his mother's death. Instead, he began teaching history at Xiuye Primary School – a position he obtained with the help of an old friend. Mao lived in the school and received a low salary (four yuan per month), but this was sufficient to pay for his food and water.

Mao's return to Changsha coincided with the anti-imperialist May Fourth Movement in Beijing. On May 4th 1919, vigorous student protests began after the Chinese government failed to defend its national interests in light of the terms drawn by the Treaty of Versailles. Germany had surrendered the port of Qingdao and the surrounding Jiaozhou Bay after the Siege of Tsingtao, and Japan was determined to gain control of the former German colony. England, Italy, and France had benefited from an allying with Japan during World War I and were relying on Japan to cooperate in an emerging war against Soviet Russia and thus supported Japan's bid for control over these areas[xx].

The patriotic students were outraged and indignant that China would only be given some ancient astronomical instruments that the Germans had taken during the Boxer Rebellion. They were also appalled at the apparent presence of Chinese traitors who would allow such humiliating concessions for private profit. A fervent anti-Japanese patriotic movement began, targeted at high-ranking government officials who were suspected of betraying national interests. On May 4th, over three thousand students arrived at Tiananmen Square with white flags (the color of mourning) to protest Japanese control over Qingdao[xxi]. When they were refused entry to the nearby Legation Quarter (with the aim of submitting a petition to the American minister), they headed over to the house of Cao Rulin, the minister of communications, to express their fury. Cao managed to escape, but Zhang Zongxiang, the Chinese minister to Tokyo, was physically assaulted by the students. Cao's house was eventually set on fire.

Their anti-Japanese sentiments resonated throughout the city during the following months. Rickshaw pullers, workers, merchants and members of the gentry demonstrated similarly patriotic feelings through strikes, demonstrations, and refusal of service to the Japanese in the country. Japanese goods were boycotted throughout China. Stores that traded and sold Japanese goods were vandalized. Mao would help organize such grassroots protest endeavors by a Hunan student association he co-organized. Cao Rulin, Zhang Zongxiang and Lu Zongyu (the director of the Chinese Mint) were forced to resign. It was only the news that Chinese delegates had declined to sign the Treaty of Versailles on June 28 that quelled the protests.

At this time, Mao decided that political propaganda would be a more effective means of informing, influencing, persuading and mobilizing the masses. Without the financial means to establish a newspaper, Mao and his comrades decided to form a Hunan-based student information journal titled *Xiangjiang pinglun* (Xiang River review). In its founding manifesto, Mao, the editor-in-chief, wrote "Unfettered by any of the old views or superstitions, we must seek the truth. In dealing with people, we advocate uniting the popular masses, and toward the oppressors, we believe in continuing the 'sincere admonishment movement.'" The oppressors he referred to include foreign imperialists such as Japan, bureaucrats, militarists, and capitalists. At this point, he believed in non-violent forms of protest, preferring the use of boycotts, strikes and peaceful protests.

Mao had been personally struck by the arrest of his intellectual idol Chen Duxiu by Beijing militarists after distributing a leaflet that contained harsh criticism of the government's domestic and foreign policies in relation to the ex-German colony. In his newly-founded journal, he attributed the arrest to critical deficits in the nation's mental faculties:

"The real danger lies in the total emptiness and rottenness of the mental universe of the entire Chinese people. Of China's 400 million people, about 390 million are superstitious. They superstitiously believe in spirits and ghosts, in fortune-telling, in fate, in despotism. There is absolutely no recognition of the individual, of the self, of truth. This is because scientific thought has not developed. In name, China is a republic, but in reality, it is an autocracy that is getting worse and worse as one regime replaces another ...[The] masses of the people haven't the faintest glimmer of democracy in their mentality and have no idea what democracy actually is[xxii]."

His attempt at publishing had been tremendously successful. By the time his fourth issue was sold on August 4, it had an initial print run of five thousand copies. Mao would write the articles, edit them, proofread and compose the printer's dummy, and occasionally even sold copies on the street. Its pages would host the article that earned him national recognition: "The Great Union of the Popular Masses." In this ambitious essay, which spanned three separate issues, Mao addressed the ultimate question that had swirled in his mind all these years: what revolutionaries of this generation should do when "the decadence of the state, the sufferings of humanity, and the darkness of society have all reached an extreme." He argued that the masses needed to unite against the aristocrats and capitalists to combat the violence of oppression and proposed that trade unions be formed to protect the interests of the poor, vulnerable and weak. Given their greater numbers, the aristocrats and capitalists would be unable to defend themselves against a mass uprising – as had occurred during the 1917 Russian Revolution[xxiii]. He also implored Chinese soldiers to switch allegiances to the popular masses and help usher in a more just society. The article was well received in the cities, with even Beijing intellectuals who had ignored him when he was a librarian's assistant lavishing praise.

Emboldened, Mao organized political activity against Zhang Jingyao, the corrupt, violent, and exploitative governor of Hunan. He was also invited by the Sino-American hospital Xiangya to serve as the editor in chief of its weekly journal *New Hunan*. As with his *Xiang River Review*, the publication of the *New Hunan* was soon halted by the authorities.

As Mao's fame and popularity grew, so did his appeal to the opposite sex. At twenty-five, he embarked on his first romantic affair. While Yang Kaihui was in Beijing, Mao pursued a romance with her father's favorite female student, Tao Yi. The two bonded over their shared passions for liberalism, democracy, and free love. Having been forced into an unwanted arranged marriage himself, Mao was a firm believer in individual choice in matters of romance and marriage[xxiv]. The two soon went separate ways, however. By 1920, Mao had begun to firmly embrace the tenets of communism. Tao Yi found herself incapable of supporting Bolshevism. She left for Shanghai soon after they broke up and founded a women's school there.

As their romance unfolded and dissolved, Mao was determined to rally opposition against Zhang. In November 1920, he held a meeting to revive the Renovation of the People Study Society. By organizing it into two clearly defined departments (a legislative and executive department) and forming an Executive Committee, the loose coalition of individuals began to resemble a centralized political party. After nearly a year of inactivity, the organization decided to hold a public burning of a significant quantity of contraband Japanese goods that they uncovered while inspecting a warehouse in Changsha. This demonstration was thwarted by Zhang's military troops, who were led by his younger brother Zhang Jingtang. His soldiers overpowered the student protesters, beat them, and forced them to vacate the town square.

Mao and his comrades decided to retaliate by organizing a national campaign to oust Zhang. Strikes began on December 6, with seventy-three out of seventy-five of the schools shutting down. Teachers and students insisted on staying away from the school until Zhang was unseated from political power in Hunan. Mao also organized a delegation to Beijing to pressure the president's administration, his cabinet and various ministers to exert their influence to punish and remove Zhang because of the corruption, theft, rape, violence, and murders he had committed. The government had no real intentions of dealing with Zhang and merely promised that a "secret investigation" was underway. Zhang would remain in power until 1920, only to have his position of governor occupied by another warlord.

He also suffered another blow while in Beijing. Upon arrival, he learnt that his beloved professor Yang Changji had been suffering from terminal stomach cancer. He met Yang Kaihui again at her father's bedside and helped to establish a fund to support his family after he died while leaving them little financial support.

Inspiration nevertheless came with news of the Bolshevik Revolution in Russia. Mao began to explore Marxist texts after learning the Bolshevik Party had been successful in unifying peasants and workers against the aristocrats and plutocrats that he resented. During this time, Mao perused abbreviated translations of the *The Communist Manifesto, The Critique of the Gotha Programme,* Vladimir Lenin's "Political Parties in Russia and the Tasks of the Proletariat", Leon Trotsky's "Manifesto of the Communist International to the Proletariat of the World", Karl Kautsky's *Class Struggle,* and Thomas Kirkup's *A History of Socialism.* The October Revolution in Russia prompted widespread interest in Marxist theories in China, but many leading intellectuals only focused on Bolshevism instead of the broader spectrum of Marxist thought. Mao was not singularly interested in Marxism, however. He also studied the works of liberal intellectuals like Henri Bergson, Bertrand Russell, John Dewey while dabbling with linguistics and Buddhism.

On April 11, 1920, Mao embarked on a journey from Beijing to Tianjin, Jinan (capital of the Shandong province), Qufu (the birthplace of Confucius), and to the summit of the holy mountain of Taishan. He visited Zoucheng (the birthplace of Mencius), before heading to Nanjing, and then to Shanghai. There, he spent half his time earning money by working as a laundryman and the other half discussing politics and walking through the city. He would have become well-acquainted with the city's cosmopolitan character, given the presence of many Europeans, Americans, Japanese, French citizens, and Russians in the International Settlement. He continued to advocate for positive political change in Hunan by advancing the idea of an "independent Hunan," freed from the rule of the northern government. When he visited his intellectual idol Chen Duxiu to discuss his ideas of secession, however, he found that Chen was being courted by Comintern agents to establish an alliance with Soviet Russia and disseminate communist ideas within China.

Left uncertain about this development, Mao returned to Hunan and decided to form a cooperative bookstore with his friends. The Cultural Book Society was meant to enrich the people of Hunan with affordable books, journals, and newspapers that advanced social and political literature. This included works by Darwin, Plato, Marxist texts, and Mao's personal favorites. The store was a success. More branches opened in seven districts across Hunan by April 1921. Within the same quarters as the bookstore, Mao founded the Russia Studies Society. Its goal was to organize the collective study of Soviet Russia, publish research and reviews of the nation and its ideology, and fund a Russian language class for those who intended to travel to Moscow for further study. Mao would learn Russian in the hopes of studying in Russia.

He also continued to advocate for an independent Hunan, but the petitions, agitation, numerous articles, meetings, and demonstrations failed to catalyze any revolution. Mao was disheartened by the passivity and apathy of the general population to the cause for reform and began to see the appeal of Bolshevism. By July 1920, Chen Duxiu was heading a communist cell in Shanghai. By August, the Shanghai Socialist Youth League had been formed. After other such organizations materialized in other cities, the Socialist Youth of China was officially announced. The nation's first communists were not workers or peasants. They were mainly students, journalists and young teachers who all aimed to emulate the Russian Revolution in their homeland as soon as the opportunity arose. Chen, the oldest member of the group, began propagating communist ideals and Marxist theory to influence fellow intellectuals as well as the workers.

Mao began to see the utility of Bolshevism at this time. His experiences with political movements on a grassroots level had left him disillusioned with the idea of everyday Chinese citizens rising above centuries of the feudal rule to engender self-government. The Bolsheviks had succeeded in Russia with a totalitarian dictatorship by the ruling communist party, which curtailed civic freedoms instead of encouraging it. At the time, 390 million (out of 400 million) of Chinese citizens were illiterate. The monarchical rule had been abolished in 1912, but they had no understanding of what living in a republic meant. Bolshevik-style communism would appeal to the masses by virtue of its ideals of universal equality, but it would simultaneously imbue the leaders of the communist party with uncontested power. Meanwhile, it would also capture the imagination of the young revolutionaries with its grand narrative of class struggle and ultimate aim of having the workers overthrow their oppressive capitalist overlords. In China, a proletariat revolution would rise against several forces: (1) the familiar feudal-militarist forces; (2) the new and emerging capitalist bourgeoisie; (3) the imperialist foreign powers who wielded foreign capital and influence in China.

When Mao was appointed as the director of a primary school that was part of the Provincial First Normal School, he gained the benefits of a considerable salary for the first time in his life. He also had access to a pool of impressionable young people he could recruit into the growing ranks of the Hunan chapter of the Socialist Youth League. He also needed to persuade the other members of the Renovation of the People Study Society to accept the tenets of Bolshevism, and thereby orient its political compass towards communism.

As Mao enjoyed steady success in convincing additional people to convert to communism, he also made a significant step in his romantic life. After Yang Changji's death, Yang Kaihui returned to Changsha with her mother and brother in January 1920 to bury his coffin where he was born (in Bancang, a small town north of Changsha). Kaihui then continued her studies in Changsha. Mao and Kaihui began a slow courtship, which involved long walks along the river. Instead of directly talking about their feelings for each other, they discussed politics, the Bolshevik revolution, and Marxist thought. Kaihui eventually joined the Socialist Youth League due to Mao's influence. In the winter of 1920, they were married. They omitted the rituals of a traditional Chinese marriage ceremony (the dowry, the red palanquin), which they deemed to be "petty bourgeois philistinism.[xxv]"

In January 1921, the Renovation of the People Study Society held an important meeting that would decide their political and ideological orientation from then on. They debated on the merits of social policy, moderate communism, anarchism, radicalism, and social democracy. They eventually agreed the Russian form of socialism would be best-suited to China since dictatorship could be used to force change onto a relatively apathetic population.

Instead of rejoicing at this momentous occasion, Mao fell into despair (possibly as a result of all the stress he had endured as he arrived at this moment). In a letter he penned to a friend at this point, he excoriated himself (a highly atypical occurrence) for all the "defects" that prevented him for becoming the great leader he had always aspired to become[xxvi]. He listed eight specific character flaws: (1) he was overly emotional; (2) he often resorted to subjective judgments;

(3) he was fairly narcissistic; (4) he was often too arrogant; (5) he seldom analyzed his own mistakes, typically blaming others when things went wrong; (6) he excelled at lofty rhetoric, but was deficient when it came to systematic analysis; (7) he had an over-inflated sense of his accomplishments; (8) his will was not as strong as he had assiduously shaped it to be. This moment of intense self-doubt did not last long.

Chapter 5 – The Communist Party of China's Growing Pains

On 29 June 1921, Mao left Changsha for Shanghai to attend the founding congress of the Chinese Communist Party (CCP[xxvii]). At this time, Sun Yat-Sen had been appointed as the president of the Republic of China – a signal that a new era was at hand. The path ahead was nevertheless far from certain. There were only fifty-three people in the CCP at this point. At the meeting, Mao Zedong was appointed as the party secretary. The core principles of the CCP were laid out during this meeting[xxviii]:

• The proletariat would stage a revolution to unseat the capitalist class, forming a new nation devoid of class distinctions.

• A dictatorship of the proletariat was to be formed to achieve the final stage of the class struggle.

• All private ownership of capital and the productive means of society (machines, factories, land, buildings, etc.) were to be replaced by social ownership.

• As a communist nation, China would unite with the Third International (also known as The Communist International), the international communist organization that advocated for world communism.

The delegates were nevertheless in conflict with the Comintern representatives who attended the meeting. They did not accept the idea that Chinese communists should be temporarily allied with the more bourgeois nationalists (i.e. Sun Yat-Sen) in organizing a national revolution. The Comintern agents in China thus had to convince their Chinese counterparts to engage the KMT (Kuomintang[xxix]) instead of attempting to stage a proletariat revolution on their own.

Like the majority of his comrades, Mao was opposed to the idea of the CCP cooperating with the KMT to achieve its goals. After returning to Changsha, Mao founded the Hunan branch of the All-China Workers' Secretariat with the aim of catalyzing a worker's movement under the influence of the CCP. With the help of local anarchists, he organized a two-thousand-worker strike in April 1921, at a cotton mill in Changsha. He convinced the two key leaders of Hunan's Labor Association of the importance of instilling a class consciousness, and they eventually joined the Socialist Youth League[xxx]. When both were executed by the thugs working for the new Hunan governor Zhao Hengti, Mao was able to assume leadership of the workers' movement in the province.

There may have only been three large industrial enterprises in the entire Hunan province, but Mao was still keen on realizing Marx's vision of a worker-led revolution. Mao considered the coolies, rickshaw pullers, and seasonal laborers to all fall under the category of "workers." As 1923 unfolded, Mao successfully organized twenty-two trade unions with the help of his comrades. They were unions for miners, railway workers, typographers, rickshaw pullers, barbers, municipal service workers, etc[xxxi]. A fervent labor movement had begun, climaxing in many strikes that aimed to increase their wages, reduce their working hours from twelve hours per day to eight hours per day, and improve their working conditions. Mao was personally involved in the organization of many of these strikes and would give rousing speeches to inspire and mobilize the miners, railroad and factory workers across the nation. He also recruited his wife, his two younger brothers, his second cousin and his second cousin's wife to join the CCP and help him stir the worker's movement onward. He appointed his middle brother Zemin to become the bursar at the primary school he directed. His younger brother Zetan was appointed as the secretary of the municipal committee of the Chinese Socialist Youth League.

The successes of many of the strikes Mao organized helped him gain major support among the workers. When the Hunan Federation of Trade Unions (HFTU) was founded on November 5, 1922, Mao was elected as its general secretary[xxxii]. With his newfound influence, Mao was able to pressure Governor Zhao Hengti to recognize the workers' constitutional rights to organize themselves and to strike. Mao and his comrades were nevertheless unsuccessful in converting the workers to communism. The vast majority of workers were apolitical, and not immediately radicalized despite participating in strikes to improve their working conditions. Mao had to rely on other means of opposing the governor.

On October 10, 1921, Mao was elected as the secretary as the Hunan committee of the CCP. When the Special Xiang District Committee formed under the dictate of the CCP's Central Bureau in May 1922, Mao was elected as secretary. He was also the head of the Socialist Youth League of Changsha's Executive Committee. He had already been serving as the general manager of the Self-Study University he founded in Changsha (after resigning from his headmaster position at the primary school he was working at) by August that year. He was beginning to monopolize the power of this underground Bolshevik movement and would exert an unparalleled influence over the newly recruited communists and socialists within the region.

In early 1922, five delegates from the First CCP Congress visited Moscow and Petrograd to attend the first Congress of the Peoples of the Far East, upon invitation from the Bolshevik leaders. There, they were persuaded to cooperate with the nationalist revolutionaries in order to emancipate the millions of struggling Chinese citizens. This time, the Russians were successful in convincing the CCP to unite with the nationalist revolutionaries in opposing the imperialists and militarists. There was some opposition, but the CCP ultimately resolved to form a temporary alliance with the KMT. They were, after all, reliant on financial support from Moscow to fund all their activities. With Sun Yat-sen's endorsement, the proletariat, the peasants, and the national bourgeoisie would thus be united in opposing foreign imperialism and the corrupt Peking government. The communists would not join the KMT and would retain their independence.

As Mao organized strikers and demonstrations in Hunan, Sun Yat-Sen and leaders of the CCP arranged meetings to discuss the structure, nature, and content of their alliance. Sun's famous Three Principles of the People (also known as the Three Great Principles) were reformulated as nationalism (self-definition for the Chinese people), socialism (people's livelihood) and democracy (the rights of the people)[xxxiii]. Sun also agreed to have the KMT mirror the CCP's alignment with Russia.

Mao became a father on October 21, 1922. He named his first son Anying, which means "The Hero Who Reaches the Shore of Socialism." He had little opportunity to care for his newborn son. On February 7, the militarist Wu Peifu initiated a bloody retaliation against the railroad workers on strike. With thirty-two workers killed, two hundred wounded and many workers' clubs and trade unions under threat, Mao was compelled to take swift and decisive action. The next day, he organized a general strike on the Changsha-Wuchang railroad as twenty thousand workers and students attended a memorial meeting for those who had been killed. Other urban trade unions organized meetings, while a major demonstration occurred at the Anyuan mines. The following month, Mao sponsored a major anti-Japanese demonstration in his capacity as the head of the Special Xiang District Committee. Over sixty thousand people marched through the streets of Changsha, demanding that Japan return the Chinese territories it had control over. In April, Hunan Governor Zhao Hengti retaliated against Mao and the union leaders. With an arrest warrant on his head, Mao was forced to escape.

His superiors in the CCP were pleased with the progress he had made and were happy to have him replicate what he had achieved in other provinces. His wife Kaihui was pregnant with his second child as he departed for Shanghai, without any inkling of when she would see him again. From Shanghai, Mao headed to Canton as the CCP's Central Executive Committee relocated. The experience of witnessing the deaths of the Hankou railway workers and Zhao Hengti's violent retaliation against the workers' movement in Hunan had convinced Mao that allying with Sun's Canton government was necessary for victory. Sun Yat-Sen's government in Canton had provided support to the Chinese workers and Hong Kong seamen who went on a similar strike, allowing them to achieve far more success than the communist-backed Hunan workers had achieved.

During the Third Congress of the Communist Party from June 12-20, 1923, Mao ultimately agreed with the majority on having the CCP help the KMT expand its support base outside of Canton. With the working class being relatively small, the CCP would not be able to become a mass organization in the immediate future. Mao was also elected as a member of the Central Executive Committee (CEC) for the first time. He was made the head of the Organizational Department and secretary of the CEC. He had risen through the ranks and was now the second in command in the party – second only to his idol Chen Duxiu. His reputation for being a capable writer, thinker, and grassroots leader had even reached Moscow. At this time, he began to envision the power that could be gained by mobilizing the landless peasants against the powerful landowners.

As the Comintern agents, the CCP and the KMT further clarified the political front they were uniting on, Mao moved to Shanghai at Chen Duxiu's request. He still supported the alliance with the KMT but was wary of the possibility of the CCP being wholly subsumed by the larger organization. At the time, he defined the political problem as "the problem of the national revolution. To use the might of the people to overthrow the warlords and to overthrow foreign imperialism, which colludes with the warlords in their evil acts – such is the historic mission of the Chinese people ... We must all have faith that the one and only way to save oneself and the nation is the national revolution[xxxiv]."

In September, Mao headed to Changsha to establish a KMT branch. His communist comrades resisted the idea, and his objective was made even more difficult when Governor Zhao Hengti declared martial law in the Hunan province. He also ordered for Mao and the other leaders of the labor movement to be arrested. Mao's second son Anqing was born at this trying time. His named means "The Youth Who Reaches the Shore of Socialism." In January 1924, Mao left his family for Shanghai once again to attend Sun Yat-Sen's Unification Congress of the KMT as a delegate from Hunan. The congress' main outcome was the formation of a united front, with the communists gaining full admission to the KMT. There were nevertheless many contradictions and points of conflict between the communists and Sun Yat-Sen's followers. Meanwhile, Mao's health had begun to deteriorate under the strain of his workload. His place of residence in the dirty, smoke-filled small town of Zhabei had also contributed to his declining health. He resigned from his position as secretary of the Organizational Department. In December that year, he requested medical leave from the CCP Central Executive Committee. Mao and his family left Shanghai for Changsha. He would spend seven months there and did not return to Shanghai to attend the Fourth Congress of the CCP, which took place in January 1925. His decision to stay out of the fray indicated his intolerance for the politicking between the communists and the "bourgeois nationalists," as well as the constant interference from Moscow. Mao was not re-elected to the new Central Executive Committee.

During his time away from the city, Mao began to spread Marxist ideas and Bolshevism among the peasants of his clan. With the help of his family members, he established over twenty peasant unions by the spring of 1925. As an intellectual, Mao saw himself as being a class above the illiterate peasants who had toiled on the land for centuries. He nevertheless relished the opportunity to rally them together and became more assured of his initial vision of having the vast peasantry lead the revolution he had been waiting for.

On March 12 that year, Sun Yat-Sen died of liver cancer in Beijing, where he was to attend a peace conference that would discuss how best to unify the country. After a brief power struggle within the KMT, the party's "leftists" prevailed. Wang Jingwei, who had been the head of the Propaganda Department of the CEC, replaced Sun as the leader of the KMT and the head of the government in Canton.

On 30th May that same year, a surge of intense nationalism erupted in Shanghai. British troops had fired at a crowd of protesters, who were agitating over the murder of Gu Zhenghong, a communist worker, by a Japanese man. Gu's murder had led to major protests and another wave of anti-Japanese sentiment, which intensified when Chinese militarists in Qingdao heeded the wishes of Japanese entrepreneurs and fired at the protesting workers, killing two of them and wounding sixteen others. The events in Qingdao catalyzed two thousand students to gather on Nanking Road, within the International Settlement, and to protest the presence of all imperial powers in the nation. The police officers ended up killing ten of them and wounding many others, causing even more agitation and fury. The death count only increased when American, Italian and British warships arrived via Huangpu River after two hundred thousand Shanghai workers went on strike. Forty-one Chinese citizens were killed and 120 were wounded[xxxv].

These events led to the May Thirtieth Movement. Nation-wide strikes, protest meetings, boycotts, demonstrations, and a mass migration of workers from the colonial centers of Shanghai, Shamian, and Hong Kong transpired. The KMT government supported these strikes by declaring a blockade of Hong Kong and Shamian and forming the Hong Kong-Shamian Strike Committee. As the revolutionary forces magnetized the entire nation, the CCP-KMT alliance began to exude a more powerful appeal.

In his home village of Shaoshan, Mao rallied the peasant unions around the cause of patriotism and anti-imperialism. Peasants were now introduced to the idea of boycotting foreign goods. When Mao organized the peasants against a local wealthy farmer named Chen, however, he prompted Governor Zhao Hengti to announce a new order for his arrest. Mao had opposed Chen's refusal to sell grain from his reserves to the peasants, who were afraid of starving due to a drought (he would be able to sell them at a greater price in the city). Mao had rallied over a hundred peasants to march to Chen's warehouse with bamboo poles and hoes, demanding to buy the grain at a fair price. Chen was forced to agree, but quickly informed Zhao of Mao's actions.

Mao fled for Changsha and then headed south to Canton. Mao had suffered a nervous attack during his trip and had to spend two weeks in Dongshan Hospital as he recovered. The news of a scandalous series of romantic betrayals within the CCP's upper echelon only worsened his condition. Kaihui's arrival in Canton with her mother and their children soon afterward helped him recuperate.

Chapter 6 – The Northern Expedition

In the earlier half of 1926, the efforts of the CCP and Comintern to exert a greater communist influence over the KMT (Chinese Nationalist Party) led to an anti-leftist military coup led by Chiang Kai-shek[xxxvi]. In March that year, Chiang would no longer pretend to be aligned with the CCP or the Soviet Union. Chiang declared martial law, had several communists arrested, and mobilized his trips to patrol the homes of many Soviet military advisers. He publicly announced his position as thus: "I believe in communism and am almost a communist myself, but the Chinese communists have sold out to the Russians and become 'their dogs.' Therefore, I oppose them[xxxvii]." Chiang's coup was peaceful, but it also firmly established a military dictatorship and compromised the positions of the communists and KMT "leftists." Chiang also demanded the political and organizational autonomy of the communists within the KMT be restricted. He began to monopolize power within the party by having himself appointed as the chairman of the Standing Committee of the Guomindang CEC, the head of the National Government's Military Council, the head of the KMT CEC's Department of Military Cadres, and the commander in chief of the National Revolutionary Army. Given that Stalin wished that the CCP remain within the KMT and bide their time, the CCP was forced to accept their diminished positions.

As a result, Mao was forced to resign from his post in the KMT CEC. He focused his energies on organizing the Chinese peasantry with his newfound position as the director of the Sixth Session of the Peasant Movement Training Institute. By then, he had gained a reputation as the foremost expert on the question of how to involve the peasantry in the revolution amongst the KMT leaders and the CCP. Through his writings, Mao advocated that the peasants, sharecroppers, farm laborers and vagrants revolt against the entire landlord class, who he deemed to be equivalent to the despised imperialists, militarists, and bureaucrats.

When March ended, Chiang had made the necessary preparations for his Northern Expedition: a military campaign to pacify the militarists in the north and to ultimately unify China[xxxviii]. Over 100,000 officers from the National Revolutionary Army headed north to engage the three groups of militarists who stood in opposition to Chiang Kai-shek: Wu Peifu, Marshal Sun Chuanfang, and Marshal Zhang Zuolin. While Wu and Sun's armies each surpassed 200,000 officers, Zhang had approximately 350,000 men. Luck was nevertheless on Chiang's side. An army division within Wu's coalition, led by commander Tang Shengzhi, had defected to Canton. Chiang mobilized his officers to rally around Tang, and the latter's officers were regrouped as the NRA's Eighth Corps.

In 1926, the NRA had achieved a major victory by assuming control of Wuhan. The National government was relocated from Canton to Wuhan. On the first day of 1927, Wuhan was declared the capital of Kuomintang China. As the NRA took over and occupied many provinces, the peasants became emboldened to act on their burgeoning class consciousness. By December 1926, the number of peasants who had joined the numerous peasant organizations available had increased from 400,000 to 1.3 million[xxxix]. They attacked and destroyed the homes of the rich landowners across the countryside, seeking revenge for the years of humiliation and exploitation that had endured at the hands of their wealthier counterparts. Anyone who owned land, however insignificant in size, was deemed to be a member of the gentry and greatly suspect. In their wake, all signs of wealth – pools filled with expensive fish, ornate furniture, artworks, and jewelry – were either destroyed or stolen. When asked to prepare a report for this unprecedented uprising, Mao condoned the excessive violence and terror as a necessary part of the revolution. Tensions within the KMT – between the communists and Chiang's "rightists" – intensified. The NRA overthrew the warlord Sun Chuanfang on March 21 and claimed Nanjing two days later.

At this time, Mao was also basking in success. His idea for a redistribution of land in the countryside – a radical suggestion – had been approved by the CCP and the KMT. In April Mao was included in the CEC's Land Committee to implement measures that would facilitate the transfer of land to the peasants. He also welcomed the birth of his third son with Kaihui. Mao named him Anlong, which meant "Dragon Who Reaches the Shore of Socialism."

The NRA eventually encountered a setback when they attacked the residence of important foreigners in Nanjing. In retaliation, the British and American ships shelled at the army. The NRA was also participating in an increasing number of conflicts with trade union organizations, and worker and peasant coalitions who had armed themselves. The peasants and workers had indiscriminately revolted against all landlords, even the medium-sized and petty ones that formed the foundation of the KMT. The NRA sought their revenge for arrested, assaulted and murdered family members against the masses, killing thousands in horrible ways. The NRA also turned on the communists. On April 28, Mao received the crushing news that Professor Li Dazhao and nineteen leaders from the Northern Bureau of the CCP had been tortured and then executed. Before long, the CCP was defeated by Chiang's forces.

As the CCP was in dire straits, it was Mao who concluded the communists would only secure power in China if it could brandish its own military force. His famed quote endures: "We must know that political power is obtained from the barrel of the gun." He recommended a strategic retreat to buy enough time to train an army of paupers, peasants, workers, and the landless. After Chen Duxiu sunk into depression when the KMT executed his eldest son, Qu Qiubai replaced him as the leader of the CCP. He agreed with Mao's suggestion that the CCP retreat into the mountains. On July 15, there would be little choice: all communists were expelled from the KMT. The communists attempted to battle the KMT soldiers with the Workers' and Peasants' Red Army of China (the "Red Army[xiii]"), but they were forced to accept defeat by September 15. They headed east, to the Jinggang Mountains in Jiangxi.

Chapter 7 – Communists at Large

Mao bid farewell to Kaihui as he departed, as she would not be following the Red Army to Jiangxi. She would head with their children and their nanny to her mother's home in Bancang instead. She would never see him again and expressed her longing for his company in a poem: "Not even a letter of even a note from you. No one to ask how you are./ If I had wings, I'd fly to see you./ To pine forever for one's love is torture. When shall we two meet again?[xli]" There, she was eventually pressured by the KMT commander to renounce her husband publicly. When she refused, she was sentenced to death on November 14, 1930.

When Mao heard the news a month later, he sent his mother-in-law thirty silver yuan for a gravestone. He somberly wrote, "The death of Kaihui cannot be repaid even should I die a hundred deaths." Mao's actions did not match his words. He had married a local interpreter, He Zizhen, only four months after leaving his wife and three sons. Like Kaihui, who had heard of Mao's remarriage two years before her execution, Zizhen (who was only eighteen when she first met Mao) would eventually learn her husband was incapable of fidelity.

Mao's refuge in Jinggang (which directly translated to "wells and ridges") housed over a thousand men and officers at the foot of the tallest mountain in the vicinity. There, he organized them into the Assembly of Workers, Peasants, and Soldier's Deputies (a legislative body) and the People's Assembly (an executive organ). By forming an alliance with the outlaws in the region, he was able to solidify his power in the region. As the KMT decimated the communists in the urban areas, many of them fled to the countryside.

His power within the CCP was nevertheless slipping. The Central Committee expelled him from their ranks for his "military opportunism," i.e. a lack of faith in the strength of the masses to accomplish the revolution. He was also dismissed from his other responsibilities in the party and demoted to the post of commander of the First Division. This left him without the power to contribute to discussions on political and military questions. His appointment as the secretary of the Hunan-Jiangxi Special Border Area Committee allowed him to monopolize power in the Jinggang region.

In May 1928, the number of communist fighters in Jinggang had grown to eighteen thousand. Mao took to the task of organizing them into disciplined soldiers. To obtain the resources needed to supply them with clothing, food, medicine, and weapons, he decided to implement a radical land redistribution scheme. He confiscated all the lands that belonged to landlords and peasants and Jinggang and then redistributed it to the rural villagers who supported the communist regime. Those who received the land were compelled to work on it. The Red Army soldiers gained more military experience as they took down the local landlords and gentry that opposed the policy.

By the end of the year, Mao and the Red Army were compelled to leave their strategic base in the mountains. All the resources in the vicinity had been used up. Many of the local villagers and industries had been decimated as people fled to escape Mao's militarized version of communism. Only six thousand soldiers remained.

Mao relocated his base to the southern province of Jiangxi, along the Jiangxi-Fujian border. They would be far from the urban centers controlled by the KMT, with a local population that was sympathetic towards the communists. KMT troops were hunting them down, prompting them to take an irregular course. The Red Army claimed to protect the interests of the workers and peasants but made exploitative demands from the merchants and rich peasants they encountered.

In May 1929, He Zizhen gave birth to Mao's first daughter. He named her Jinhua ("Gold Flower"), and then insisted she hand her over to a peasant family for fifteen yuan. He promised Zizhen they would be able to find her after the revolution, but they would never see her again.

Mao's Red Army was dwindling, but he was able to make the most of his soldiers by perfecting his guerilla tactics. Militarized communists would adopt these successful military tactics in many other Asian, African and South American countries. By using them deftly, Mao was able to resist the KMT soldiers and antagonize opposing locals. He was able to implement his land redistribution policy in Jiangxi, as he had done in Jinggang. The Red Army destroyed tax offices and killed tax collectors alongside the gentry, officials, KMT members, priests, missionaries and the militarists.

On October 4, 1930, Mao took control over the Ji'an, a commercial city in Jiangxi, and announced the formation of the Jiangxi Provincial Soviet Government[xlii]. The Red Army obtained significant funds from the rich townspeople and were able to settle comfortably in the area. Mao's military successes had earned him the approval of Stalin, who saw the Red Army as being crucial for a communist victory in China.

The communists in Jiangxi soon began engaging in infighting, as the native people of Jiangxi viewed the Red Army as outsiders and opposed Mao's radical land reforms. By the end of October, Mao's Red Army would execute over a thousand Jiangxi communists. Before long, Mao also had to contend with increased aggression from the KMT army. His guerilla tactics ("the enemy advances, we retreat; the enemy camps, we harass; the enemy tires, we attack; the enemy retreats, we pursue[xliii]") were nevertheless able to defeat the KMT's first two attempts to encircle and annihilate the Red Army. Chiang Kai-shek himself would eventually be compelled to travel to Jiangxi and lead the charge against the communists.

When the Japanese began pursuing an increasingly comprehensive expansionist policy in the region, however, Chiang was forced to retreat from Jiangxi. The Japanese occupied Mukden, Manchuria's largest city, on September 18, 1931[xliv]. With their formidable discipline and weapons, they assumed control of the entirety of Manchuria and its population of thirty million people by late fall. In the meantime, Mao solidified his power over the region and worked to redirect the wave of anti-Japanese fervor against Chiang, who had not defended Manchuria against the Japanese. He was now facing not only Chiang's forces, but also opponents within the party, class enemies that opposed communism, and comrades who disagreed with or opposed him. Mao announced that the Soviet government of China had officially declared war against the Japanese (even though the communist armies were nowhere near Manchuria and Shanghai). This propaganda was nevertheless effective in creating an image of genuine nationalism for the communists.

With its increasing popularity and mass support, the Red Army was eventually able to exert control over a population of 3 million people. Mao could pursue his land reform program, besides organizing education programs and introducing measures to recruit more women to join the CCP.

Chapter 8 – The Long March

Chiang deemed the communists to be a greater threat than the encroaching Japanese. In the years between 1930 and 1934, he would rally no less than five different military encirclement campaigns with the aim of eradicating the pesky communists once and for all. In his fifth encirclement campaign, he managed to deliver a devastating blow to the communist forces by personally mobilizing 700,000 of his men and forming a series of fortifications (in the form of cement blockhouses) around communist positions.

Mao's leadership had been revoked by the CCP's Central Committee in early 1934, resulting in the Red Army abandoning his preferred guerrilla warfare strategy. This was a near-fatal mistake: many communist soldiers were lost after they attempted to face the larger and better-equipped KMT army with positional warfare strategies. The communists were forced to flee for their lives in October. At the beginning of the march, 86,000 male and female communists in Jiangxi (soldiers and administrative personnel) broke through the weakest points of the KMT encirclement and headed towards the west. Zizhen accompanied Mao, but they had to leave their newborn son Anhong with Zizhen's sister He Yi. They would never see him again.

In the beginning, they were forced to contend with multiple attacks from Chiang's ground troops, as well as constant bombardment from his air force. By the time they arrived in Zunyi, in the southwestern province of Guizhou, their morale had plunged, and the Red Army had lost more than half of its ranks. Mao had not been in charge during the beginning of the retreat, but he gained enough support to establish his uncontested dominance of the party in January 1935.

He rallied the remaining troops to head toward the northwest, to gain the security of being closer to the security border. This would also mean the communists would be near the Japanese-occupied territory in northeastern China. In June, Mao's forces merged with the communist troops that had been operating in the Sichuan-Shaanxi border area under the leadership of Zhang Guotao[xlv]. This led to a power struggle between Mao and Zhang for control of the central army in northern Sichuan. The main army eventually split into two factions, with Zhang's section heading towards the southwest. Mao led most of the troops towards northern Shaanxi, where there was a communist base to welcome them.

When he arrived there in October 1935, only 8,000 people had survived the march[xlvi]. Many had died from fighting the KMT, starvation and from diseases. Some had abandoned the march to rally the peasants along the way. Mao would proclaim his troops had covered 12,500 km, but British historians have argued they travelled only 6,000 km[xlvii]. In any case, Mao and his troops had to navigate some of the most challenging trails in the world, taking them across 18 mountain ranges and 24 rivers. They also had to contend with Chiang's forces nearly every step of the way, although they did not have to face the force of the entire KMT army (which was preoccupied with the Japanese Occupation before the March began).

The CCP was happy to capitalize on the compelling heroism that was attributed to the Long March. News of the communists' epic struggle to resist the KMT inspired many young Chinese men and women to travel to Shaanxi to enlist in Mao's Red Army. When the Japanese withdrew from China after their defeat in World War II (1939-45) to the United States, the CCP confronted the KMT once again. In 1949, the KMT was decisively defeated. Mao heralded the founding of the People's Republic of China on October 1, 1949[xlviii].

Chapter 9 – The People's Republic of China

The CCP was happy to capitalize on the compelling heroism that was attributed to the Long March. News of the communists' epic struggle to resist the KMT inspired many young Chinese men and women to travel to Shaanxi to enlist in Mao's Red Army.

His early years at the helm of the country were a great success. During this time, the CCP steered the country towards economic growth and greater political strength[xlix]. After years of military rule under the warlords, the KMT army, and the Red Army, the people of China could finally live under civilian rule. Mao's effective leadership of the CCP during the early years was critical in establishing widespread confidence in its ability to govern the nation.

In October 1950, the PLA troops (the Chinese People's Volunteers) participated in the Korean War[l] against the forces of the UN. The "Resist America, aid Korea" campaign was effective in stirring patriotism across the nation, besides restoring confidence in the nation's military capacities after decades of military humiliation by the foreign imperialists. Troops were also dispatched to Tibet during this time after the Tibetans rebelled against the consolidation of Chinese rule. Meanwhile, the CCP consolidated their power within the country by authorizing police action against political adversaries, anti-communists, bandits, and groups of people who opposed the CCP's political dominance.

After experimenting with land reform in Jianggang and Jianxi, Mao finally had the opportunity to enforce it across the entire nation. The Agrarian Reform Law of 1950 effectively destroyed the feudal and semi-feudal class by confiscating their land and redistributing it to the peasants. Land was also seized from foreign ownership, severely diminishing the power of numerous private industrialists. Despite these radical measures, the CCP was able to propel economic growth by reducing urban inflation, creating a more disciplined labor force, and securing the confidence of the capitalists (who surprisingly began to see communist rule as being "good for business"). The introduction of a marriage law and trade-union law also helped to solidify the CCP's reputation for bringing bold reforms to the nation.

The early years of the People's Republic of China were nevertheless not free from conflict and strife. The Suppression of Counterrevolutionaries campaign inflicted violence on the former KMT leaders, the heads of secret societies, religious, and religious authorities. The Three-Antis campaign decimated the communists who had been perceived as fraternizing too closely with the nation's capitalists. The capitalists themselves were subjected to The Five-Antis campaign, which compelled obedience to the CCP via charges of tax evasion, bribery, theft of state property and dishonesty when entering into contractual obligations with the government contracts. University professors were not spared either. Mao had benefited from access to the Western liberal tradition, but the new generation would be exposed only to Soviet intellectual discourse.

In 1953, Mao launched his First Five-Year Plan[i] to promote the nation's rapid industrialization. This plan was based on the Soviet experience; the CCP benefited from financial assistance and technical expertise on how to plan and execute ambitious goals while remaining true to Stalinist economic priorities. Over eighty percent of China's population lived in the rural areas, but the CCP government invested over eighty percent of its budget into the urban economy. Heavy industry was significantly promoted over agriculture, which was mostly undeveloped. The CCP began promoting voluntary forms of agricultural collectivization in the rural areas, ushering in the development of small collectives that consisted of between 20-30 households. Tensions developed between the land-owning peasants (who were forced to surrender the land they owned to the collectives without any financial benefits) and the landless peasants (who were more receptive to the collectivistic model). Many also resisted the central government's policies of extracting agricultural surpluses from the countryside to pay for the nation's investments in capital equipment, and to feed a growing urban population.

In the urban centers of industry and commerce, the capitalists and private merchants were pressured to combine their individually-owned enterprises with the state. This was part of Mao's plan to engender a "socialist transformation" of China's industries and businesses. After facing the terror of the Five-Antis campaign, many capitalists were willing to cooperate with the government to resume the operation of their businesses. In any case, the government had gained monopoly control over the banking sector that the capitalists were forced to rely on to keep making profits. As the nation's agriculture, commerce, and industry underwent a socialist transformation, its urban population grew from 77 million in 1953 to 99.5 million in 1957.

This pattern of migration created a problem for the CCP. The nation's agricultural sector was not developing fast enough to generate the surplus capital needed to feed the increasing number of workers in the urban centers or to be reinvested to modernize farming methods further. This would contribute to the disastrous food shortages of the Great Leap Forward. The financial assistance provided by the Soviet Union also had to be paid back. Finally, the development of the nation's economy required the participation of individuals with technical expertise (i.e. the nation's intelligentsia). Unlike the peasants and the capitalists, the intellectuals were not readily brought into the party line.

When Mao introduced the "Hundred Flowers" campaign[lii] in 1956 ("Let a hundred flowers blossom, a hundred schools of thought contend," the objective was help convert the nation's intellectuals to communism. Instead, they began to critique the principles of communism, the CCP, and the Chinese government. They would pay dearly for openly voicing their dissent when Mao retaliated with a vicious anti-rightist campaign.

Chapter 10 – The Great Leap Forward

In 1958, Mao initiated his second Five Year Plan (1958 - 1963) to modernize China's agriculture and industries and allow it to catch up with its American counterpart[liii]. This plan, which was named the Great Leap Forward, aimed to leapfrog the more typical process of industrialization, where businesses slowly accumulated the capital needed to invest in expensive and sophisticated machinery that would improve on efficiency and production rates. Unlike the Soviet Union, however, China had a denser population and no surplus of agricultural produce that could be converted into capital. Mao decided that China should industrialize rapidly by tapping into the sheer size of its labor force and eschew the traditional reliance on machine-centered industrial processes.

That year, an experimental commune[liv] was established in the north-central province of Henan. Each commune would house approximately 5,000 families that owned no private property, tools, or livestock. Everything was owned and managed by the commune. It provided members with food, schools, entertainment, nurseries for the young, healthcare, and "retirement homes" for the elderly who could no longer work. Each sub-division oversaw specific duties and tasks. Soldiers worked alongside the people, while CCP members ensured all decisions made were compliant with the party's ideology. The goal was to ultimately accelerate the development of China's agriculture and industries through this form of centralized economic planning. When 1958 ended, the CCP had successfully placed 700 million people into 26,578 communes across the nation.

The major problem with the commune system was that political beliefs and a dogmatic insistence on ideological purity triumphed over common sense and working expertise. Everyone was zealously encouraged to exceed the targets that had been set for them through the use of sheer hard work and determination. This zeal is most evident in the establishment of development of small backyard steel furnaces in every village and urban neighborhood, which collectively contributed to the nation's annual steel production. At the very beginning, the Great Leap Forward campaign seemed to be working. Major increases in the production of steel, coal, grain, cotton, timber, and cement were recorded. The quality of the steel produced in such conditions, however, was dubious.

By the following year, the catastrophic failure of the Great Leap Forward was evident. The farm machinery that had been produced haphazardly fell apart when they were used. The low-quality steel that was used to construct new buildings ensured they did not hold up for long. (The steel that had been produced by all the backyard furnaces across the nation was too substandard to even be used for construction). Overworked and suffering from insufficient sleep, thousands of workers were injured while working. These technical and managerial oversights were compounded by the Soviet Union withdrawing financial support for China, as well as three consecutive years of natural disasters. After excellent weather conditions in 1958, the nation suffered floods and droughts in the following years.

The diversion of a significant section of the workforce to small-scale industrial production and the inefficiency of the commune system with regards to agricultural production meant there was an insufficient surplus of food to make up for food shortage caused by the three years of natural disasters. The estimates for the exact number of Chinese citizens who died because of the disastrous The Great Leap Forward vary, but a 2010 estimate based on recently declassified documents placed the total death count at a staggering 45 million people[iv].

Starvation, malnutrition, and illness claimed the majority of the lives lost during the Great Famine of 1958 to 1962. Between 2 to 3 million of those who died lost their lives to relatively trivial infractions. When commune leaders argued with CCP officials that the goals set for their commune were impossible, they would be charged with being a "bourgeois reactionary" and imprisoned. Regular workers who were suspected of being ideological traitors, or of simply not working hard enough, could be beaten, hung, or drowned in ponds. Other punishments included being forced to eat feces and being mutilated.

When food was rationed during the famine, starvation became a common form of punishment.

Mao himself was comfortably ensconced in Zhongnanhai, Beijing. How did he react to reports of millions of Chinese people starving to death (with some resorting to cannibalism) in the countryside? In March 1959, he ordered CCP officials to take ownership of up to one-third of all the grain available, a greater portion than ever before. Meeting minutes indicate that he was indifferent to their suffering: "When there is not enough to eat people starve to death. It is better to let half of the people die so that the other half can eat their fill[lvi]."

He had to admit the program had been a horrendous failure. He did not readily accept the blame for its shortcomings, however. Given his popularity with the masses, Mao could not be easily displaced. He remained the Chairman of the CCP but resigned from his position as Head of State. Liu Shaoqi, Zhou Enlai, and Deng Xiaoping stepped in to govern the nation, and they decided to abandon the Great Leap Forward in 1960. The communes were reduced to a smaller size, private ownership of the land was reintroduced, and peasants were incentivized by the possibility selling any surplus food they produced. Meanwhile, an internal division brewed within the CCP. One division believed that the Great Leap forward failed because of implementation (i.e. bureaucratic failures and mismanagement), while the other group opined that China needed to place a higher priority on technical expertise and material incentives to spur the economy onward.

Chapter 11 – The Cultural Revolution

Mao was not content with the prospect of losing political power and control in the Chinese government, or with the possibility of being reduced to a symbolic figurehead. The nation's alliance with the Soviet Union had also deteriorated. Mao witnessed Stalin's denunciation by Nikita Khrushchev in 1956, as well as Khrushchev's removal from power in 1964. When he saw Wu Han's play "Hai Rui Dismissed from Office[lvii]" – which featured a Ming dynasty official who dared to criticize the emperor – he interpreted it as a coded means of undermining his authority and proclaiming support for defense minister Peng Dehuai[lviii], who had been dismissed after openly confronting Mao about the failures of The Great Leap Forward at the 1959 Lushan Conference[lix].

He was also concerned that "bourgeois" elements were gaining influence within the CCP, government, and society at large. Everything was at stake: his influence, power, and position within the party and the legacy of his vision of communism in the country. The Cultural Revolution[lx] was presented as a nation-wide means of purging the nation of all "bourgeois" and "reactionary" elements, who were labelled as "class enemies" and traitors to communist ideals.

In 1965, Wu Han's play was investigated, publicly denounced and banned for its "reactionary" political nature. This would establish a precedent for the radicalization of all art forms under the Cultural Revolution, effectively censoring all forms of expression – music, cinema, plays, fiction, nonfiction, poetry, visual arts – and replacing them with pro-Mao propaganda. Mao formally detailed his concerns about "bourgeois" infiltrators in a CCP Central Committee document on May 16, 1966. In August that year, the Cultural Revolution was launched across the nation at the Eleventh Plenum of the Eighth Central Committee.

The Cultural Revolution was a grand bid to secure power for Mao and his supporters within the CCP, but it also had widespread effects across the entire Chinese society. Mao had the support of radicalized youths (who formed the feared "Red Guards[lxi]") that hung on fervently to his rhetoric, and they were ready to inflict violence on anyone deemed to be a traitor to his ideals. Nothing was sacred or spared, as the Red Guards have been urged to annihilate the "four olds" wherever they encountered them: old ideas, customs, habits, and culture[lxii]. Red Guard divisions were formed in university campuses and classrooms across the nation, and they took to the task of destroying their educational institutions, churches, shrines, shops, private homes, and libraries. On 5 August 1966, the first known death by torture occurred[lxiii]. The Red Guards kicked, trampled and poured boiling water over the headmistress of a prominent girls' school in Peking. She was made to transport heavy bricks as the Red Guards assaulted her with leather belts and wooden sticks embedded with nails. The Red Guards were not asked to curtail their violence when news of her death reached the CCP.

Mao had published his infamous "Little Red Book" (*Quotations from Chairman Mao Tse-tung*) in 1964 and wielded it as a massively influential propaganda tool across the nation. The Red Guards used his quotations to organize their ideals and actions, and it became the nation's undisputed bestseller as so many other local and foreign publications were banned for containing "reactionary" elements. The Little Red Book was ubiquitous in China throughout the Cultural Revolution. Its sales surpassed even that of the Bible during the 1960s, with over a billion copies printed. Mao was easily China's bestselling author for a decade, making millions while everyone else with riches to their name was suspect.

By 1967, the Red Guards and Mao loyalists had ousted many of the influential CCP leaders who had opposed or criticized Mao. Former President Liu Shaoqi[lxiv] was expelled from the party in 1968. He died the following year after enduring brutal treatment during his arrest. Deng Xiaoping was also stripped of his power and position in the party, but he survived the Cultural Revolution and would eventually return to power after Mao's death. China's current president Xi Jinping's father, CCP veteran Xi Zhongxun, was also purged from the party, publicly humiliated and forced into exile during the Cultural Revolution.

By 1968, millions of urban youths (including a teenage Xi Jinping) were sent to the countryside to toil alongside the peasants. As older intellectuals, artisans, and professionals like doctors, lawyers and businessmen suffered verbal and physical abuse, the country's urban economy and industrial production was stifled by anarchy and chaos. The Red Guards had also begun to engage in rivalries and conflicts with one another, with each proclaiming themselves to be the singularly genuine adherent to Mao's ideals. Disillusioned with their inability to form a unified front, Mao sent most of them to toil in the countryside, restoring some semblance of order to the cities.

It is difficult to ascertain the exact number of lives lost during the Cultural Revolution, but a 2011 estimate places the number of people who died during this period to fall somewhere between 500, 000 to 8 million[lxv]. Tens of millions of people, however, were estimated to have been persecuted and harassed during this turbulent period. Economic output was curtailed, but the nation also suffered cultural losses that cannot be quantified. The nation's rich tradition of literature and fine arts that had been cultivated over centuries were dismissed overnight as being feudalistic, bourgeois, revisionist and imperialistic. Mao Yu Run, a professor of music who lived through the Cultural Revolution, recalls the inescapable cult of personality that Mao propagated throughout the nation during this period:

> "From then on, in a country of one billion people, we could only hear two voices, the voice of Mao, that hovered in our territorial sky of 9,600,000 square kilometers, and the voice of one billion people singing in unison the hymn praising Mao: "Mao, dear Mao. I march on where ever your big hand points; I do whatever I am told; I am a tamed instrument of the Party[lxvi]."

The Cultural Revolution would finally end with Mao's death on September 9, 1976, at the age of 82[lxvii]. By now, the population at large had become disillusioned with his ideals and the leadership of the CCP. Despite all the propaganda, they could see these principles and philosophies were a smokescreen for the blatant power plays that were occurring within the party lines. Even then, Mao's image was too central to the CCP for his successors to tarnish it. The Gang of Four - Mao's third wife Jiang Qing[lxviii], Wang Hongwen, Zhang Chunqiao, and Yao Wenyuan – were publicly blamed for all the losses suffered during the Cultural Revolution and were purged from the party. Deng Xiaoping would return to power after Mao's death and implement many economic reforms that aimed to repair the damage inflicted by the misguided policies of the era. It would take decades to repair the nation's educational system, and the individuals who had their schooling disrupted by the radical revolutionary fervor of the time became a "lost generation," unable to find their footing in the era of pragmatic economic growth that Deng spearheaded[lxix].

Chapter 12 – What Did Maoism Stand For?

Frank Dikötter, a Dutch historian with a specialization in modern China, has argued that the tumultuous decades of the Great Leap Forward and Cultural Revolution effectively erased the faith that the Chinese population once had in Mao's ideals: "Even before Mao died, people buried Maoism[lxx]."

Mao's image may remain in China, but the calamities it faced during his life would ironically engender an acceptance of the market reforms that Deng Xiaoping introduced. But what is Maoism? Mao was informed by Marx and Lenin's ideas, as well as the model of communism the Soviets adopted. He nevertheless believed that it was the rural peasantry that would form the revolutionary masses, instead of the urban workers[lxxi]. Maoism placed more importance on the peasant masses and viewed urban industrialization with much distrust. From his perspectives, the industrialists were also prone to be swayed by the kind of bourgeois elitism he despised. This ideal is best embodied by the backyard furnaces that were ubiquitous during The Great Leap Forward. Maoism also holds that a socialist population is always under threat from the re-emergence of bourgeois values and must be continuously re-educated and purged to retain socialist purity.

After Mao's death, Maoism would inspire revolutionaries in other nations with sizable rural populations and a history of imperial exploitation. The Nepalese rebels and the Naxalites in India are arguably the last descendants of Maoism. The Khmer Rouge is perhaps the most notorious proponents of Maoism, having killed 1.7 million Cambodians during the anti-urban purges in the 1970s.

Mao's teachings influenced revolutionaries in several nations with large rural populations, but the Nepalese insurgency is perhaps the last Maoist movement left. The "ultra-Maoist" Khmer Rouge, whose anti-urban purges in the 1970s left at least 1.7 million Cambodians dead, has essentially disappeared. And save for one tiny faction, Peru's

Maoist Shining Path has dissolved since the arrest of its founder, Abimael Guzman (aka "President Gonzalo"), in 1992.

Was Mao himself a true Maoist? Jung Chang, a Chinese-born British writer whose international bestseller *Wild Swans* (1952) is banned in China, has argued that Mao did not abide by the tenets of hard work, frugality, and abstinence that he forced on the entire population after he rose to power. Mao presented himself with simplicity in terms of clothes (i.e. the ubiquitous Mao suit), but Chang notes that he indulged in a gourmet's diet, had no less than 50 estates to his name, and was regularly entertained by young girls and courtesans. Li Zhisui, Mao's private physician from 1955 to 1976, supported Chang's description of Mao as a decadent tyrant in his memoir *The Private Life of Chairman Mao* (1988).

Conclusion

It is difficult to arrive at a definitive evaluation of Mao's legacy in China due to his long career and the sheer scale of his successes and failures. Mao's legacy as a shrewd military tactician cannot be denied: it was his guerrilla warfare tactics that allowed the CCP to survive the Nationalists and eventually defeat them. After decades of humiliation and exploitation by foreign and local oppressors, the Chinese people turned to Mao for his ability to restore pride, dignity, and confidence in the strength of the Chinese society.

If Mao had resigned from power and influence shortly after announcing the formation of the People's Republic of China, he would have retired as a national hero. His insistence on remaining in power for as long as he could, however, left him with a tainted legacy. As an administrator of the nation, he did successfully attempt to halt the excesses and inefficiencies of the bureaucracy, promote self-reliance within the people and promote the nation's industrialization. His revolutionary zeal was nevertheless less suited to governing the nation. Even now, it is hard for people to gain a tangible sense of the sheer trauma and millions of deaths that were lost during the Great Leap Forward and the Cultural Revolution. Mao's own body is preserved for perpetuity, but there are no monuments, memorials or sculptures to commemorate the millions of Chinese citizens who starved to death or those who were murdered upon accusations of being "bourgeois" or "reactionary."

How do we judge Mao as a person? His physician Li Zishui described him as "a merciless tyrant who crushed anybody who disobeyed him[lxxii]." Mao's sheer will to power was undoubtedly unquestionable. How else would the son of a peasant rise through the ranks of the Chinese Communist Party to become its most indispensable symbol? He certainly earned many opponents and adversaries within the CCP, but his ability to build loyal alliances with powerful party members and the Russians ensured that he returned to power after being repeatedly ousted. This was a man who established a cult of personality over the largest population in the world (one-quarter of the world' population) for several decades – the thought of purging Mao from China appears unthinkable.

Dr. Li has also raised the possibility that Mao was not genuinely capable of love, friendship or warmth for others. Dr. Li notes that Mao had announced, during a 1957 speech in Moscow, that he was willing to lose half of China's population (300 million people). When millions of his countrymen did start starving to death during the famine, his evident lack of empathy and concern mirrored his earlier proclamations. Erstwhile allies and followers were similarly disposed or abandoned once they had become disillusioned with the man behind the myth.

With Mao, it is also essential to make a distinction between the words and the deeds. Mao is famed for his emphasis on gender equality via his statement "Women hold up half the sky." Mao's policies encouraged women to participate in political life, in the fields, and in the factories. In the propaganda of the era, women were presented as "iron women" who performed "masculine" labor at the steel furnaces while ensuring their domestic responsibilities were well taken care of. There were nevertheless glass ceilings: no woman has ever been appointed to the Politburo standing committee[lxxiii].Similar glass ceilings existed in the urban workplaces and rural areas where women struggled to fulfill both their professional and domestic responsibilities[lxxiv]. Mao himself did not treat his wives as true equals and was never faithful to any of them.

It is difficult to reduce Mao to the figure of a monster or a hero. One could make the case that he was a severely flawed person who made indispensable contributions to the nation. Even if they disagree with his policies and their outcomes, some look to his anti-elitism and emphasis of equality as an important ideal in today's income-stratified society. Others dismiss any notion of Mao as being benevolent or well-intentioned, arguing that he is the most Machiavellian leader of the twentieth century, who hypocritically wielded ideologies and policies for the sake of consolidating and perpetuating his power[lxxv]. In any case, China's present ruler Xi Jinping has proclaimed that a total denunciation of Mao would cause chaos and strip the CCP of its legitimacy. As Mao's old enemy class – the intelligentsia – adopt an increasingly negative view of his actions, the state-owned media attempt to defend him. Mao's portraits may be absent from official CCP functions and meetings, but it will take a drastic development or a long time before China can disown his legacy.

If you enjoyed this book, then I'd really appreciate it if you would post a short review on Amazon. I read all the reviews myself so that I can continue to provide books that people want.

Check out another book by Captivating History

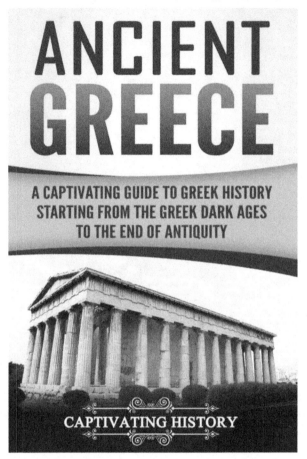

ANCIENT GREECE

A CAPTIVATING GUIDE TO GREEK HISTORY STARTING FROM THE GREEK DARK AGES TO THE END OF ANTIQUITY

CAPTIVATING HISTORY

Free Bonus from Captivating History (Available for a Limited time)

Hi History Lovers!

Now you have a chance to join our exclusive history list so you can get your first history ebook for free as well as discounts and a potential to get more history books for free! Simply visit the link below to join.

Captivatinghistory.com/ebook

Also, make sure to follow us on Facebook, Twitter and Youtube by searching for Captivating History.

Primary and Secondary Sources for The Cultural Revolution

[1] Buruma, Ian. "Cult of the Chairman." March 2001. *The Guardian.* https://www.theguardian.com/world/2001/mar/07/china.features11. Accessed 10 February 2018.

[1] "Deng Xiaoping." *Encyclopædia Britannica.* hhttps://www.britannica.com/biography/Deng-Xiaoping. Accessed 10 February 2018.

[1] Oakley, Barbara. *Evil Genes: Why Rome Fell, Hitler Rose, Enron Failed, and My Sister Stole My Mother's Boyfriend.* 2007.

[1] Rummel, R. J. "The Holocaust in Comparative and Historical Perspective". *IDEA.* April 1998. http://www.ideajournal.com/articles.php?id=17. Accessed 10 February 2018.

[1] Kristof, Nicholas D. "Legacy of Mao Called 'Great Disaster." *The New York Times.* February 1989. http://www.nytimes.com/1989/02/07/world/legacy-of-mao-called-great-disaster.html. Accessed 10 February 2018.

[1] Pantsov, Alexander and Levine, Steven I. *Mao: The Real Story.* 2012.

[1] Ibid.

[1] Chang, Jung and Halliday, Jon. *Mao: The Unknown Story.* 2005.

[1] Snow, Edgar. *Red Star over China.* 1937.

[1] Pantsov, Alexander and Levine, Steven I. *Mao: The Real Story.* 2012.

[1] Ibid.

[1] Ibid.

[1] "Changsha." *Encyclopædia Britannica.* https://www.britannica.com/place/Changsha. Accessed 10 February 2018.

[1] "Sun Yat-sen." *Encyclopædia Britannica.* https://www.britannica.com/biography/Sun-Yat-sen. Accessed 10 February 2018.

[1] Pantsov, Alexander and Levine, Steven I. *Mao: The Real Story.* 2012.

[1] Snow, Edgar. *Red Star over China.* 1937.

[1] Pantsov, Alexander and Levine, Steven I. *Mao: The Real Story.* 2012.

[1] Ibid.

[1] Schram, Stuart Reynolds. *Mao's Road to Power vol. 1: Pre-Marxist Period, 1912-20.* 1992.

[1] Pantsov, Alexander and Levine, Steven I. *Mao: The Real Story.* 2012.

[1] Ibid.

[1] "May Fourth Movement." *Encyclopædia Britannica.* https://www.britannica.com/event/May-Fourth-Movement. Accessed 10 February 2018

[1] Schram, Stuart Reynolds. *Mao's Road to Power vol. 1: Pre-Marxist Period, 1912-20.* 1992.

[1] "Russian Revolution of 1917." *Encyclopædia Britannica.* https://www.britannica.com/event/Russian-Revolution-of-1917. Accessed 10 February 2018.

[1] Chang, Jung and Halliday, Jon. *Mao: The Unknown Story.* 2005.

[1] Pantsov, Alexander and Levine, Steven I. *Mao: The Real Story.* 2012.

[1] Schram, Stuart Reynolds. *Mao's Road to Power vol. 1: Pre-Marxist Period, 1912-20.* 1992.

[1] "Chinese Communist Party." *Encyclopædia Britannica.* https://www.britannica.com/topic/Chinese-Communist-Party. Accessed 10 February 2018.

[1] Ch'en, Kung-po. *The Communist Movement in China: An Essay Written in 1924.* 1966.

[1] "Nationalist Party." *Encyclopædia Britannica.* https://www.britannica.com/topic/Nationalist-Party-Chinese-political-party. Accessed 10 February 2018.

[1] Pantsov, Alexander and Levine, Steven I. *Mao: The Real Story.* 2012.

[1] Snow, Edgar. *Red Star over China.* 1937.

[1] Pantsov, Alexander and Levine, Steven I. *Mao: The Real Story.* 2012.

[1] "Three Principles of the People." *Encyclopædia Britannica.* https://www.britannica.com/event/Three-Principles-of-the-People. Accessed 10 February 2018.

[1] Schram, Stuart Reynolds. *Mao's Road to Power vol. 2: National Revolution and Social Revolution, December 1920-June 1927.* 1992.

[1] Pantsov, Alexander and Levine, Steven I. *Mao: The Real Story.* 2012.

[1] "Chiang Kai-shek". *Encyclopædia Britannica.* https://www.britannica.com/biography/Chiang-Kai-shek. Accessed 10 February 2018.

[1] Ibid.

[1] "Northern Expedition". *Encyclopædia Britannica.* https://www.britannica.com/event/Northern-Expedition. Accessed 10 February 2018.

[1] Mao, Zedong. *Selected Works of Mao Tse-Tung: Volume 1.* 1965.

[1] "People's Liberation Army". *Encyclopædia Britannica.* https://www.britannica.com/topic/Peoples-Liberation-Army-Chinese-army. Accessed 10 February 2018.

[1] Chang, Jung and Halliday, Jon. *Mao: The Unknown Story.* 2005.

[1] "Jiangxi Soviet". *Encyclopædia Britannica.* https://www.britannica.com/topic/Jiangxi-Soviet. Accessed 10 February 2018.

[1] Mao, Zedong. "Respectfully Quoted: A Dictionary of Quotations." *Bartleby.* http://www.bartleby.com/73/1933.html. Accessed 10 February 2018.

[1] "Mukden Incident". *Encyclopædia Britannica.* https://www.britannica.com/event/Mukden-Incident. Accessed 10 February 2018.

[1] "Long March". *Encyclopædia Britannica.* https://www.britannica.com/event/Long-March. Accessed 10 February 2018.

[1] Ibid.

[1] Lau, Mimi. "The Long March: What it was and why it Matters to China's Xi Jinping." *South China Morning Post.* October 2016. http://www.scmp.com/news/china/policies-politics/article/2039033/long-march-what-it-was-and-why-it-matters. Accessed 10 February 2018.

[1] "Establishment of the People's Republic". *Encyclopædia Britannica.* https://www.britannica.com/place/China/Establishment-of-the-Peoples-Republic. Accessed 10 February 2018.

[1] "Reconstruction and Consolidation, 1949–52". *Encyclopædia Britannica.* https://www.britannica.com/place/China/Reconstruction-and-consolidation-1949-52. Accessed 10 February 2018.

[1] "Korean War." *Encyclopædia Britannica.* https://www.britannica.com/event/Korean-War. Accessed 10 February 2018.

[1] "First Five-Year Plan." *Encyclopædia Britannica.* https://www.britannica.com/topic/First-Five-Year-Plan-Chinese-economics. Accessed 10 February 2018.

[1] "Hundred Flowers Campaign." *Encyclopædia Britannica.* https://www.britannica.com/event/Hundred-Flowers-Campaign. Accessed 10 February 2018.

[1] "Commune." *Encyclopædia Britannica.* https://www.britannica.com/topic/commune-Chinese-agriculture. Accessed 10 February 2018.

[1] "Great Leap Forward." *Encyclopædia Britannica.* https://www.britannica.com/event/Great-Leap-Forward. Accessed 10 February 2018.

[1] Dikötter, Frank. "Mao's Great Leap to Famine." *The New York Times.* December 2010. http://www.nytimes.com/2010/12/16/opinion/16iht-eddikotter16.html?mtrref=undefined&gwh=B68D2BA84DBA7794C6E54CBC9EB5EC30&gwt=pay&assetType=opinion. Accessed 10 February 2018.

[1] Ibid.

[1] "Hai Rui Dismissed From Office." *Encyclopædia Britannica.* https://www.britannica.com/topic/Gang-of-Four#ref213744. Accessed 10 February 2018.

[1] "Peng Dehuai." *Encyclopædia Britannica.* https://www.britannica.com/biography/Peng-Dehuai. Accessed 10 February 2018.

[1] "Gang of Four." *Encyclopædia Britannica.* https://www.britannica.com/topic/Hai-Rui-Dismissed-From-Office. Accessed 10 February 2018.

[1] "Cultural Revolution." *Encyclopædia Britannica.* https://www.britannica.com/event/Cultural-Revolution. Accessed 10 February 2018.

[1] "Liu Shaoqi." *Encyclopædia Britannica.* https://www.britannica.com/biography/Liu-Shaoqi. Accessed 10 February 2018.

[1] Phillips, Tom. "The Cultural Revolution: All You Need to Know about China's Political Convulsion." *The Guardian.* May 2016. https://www.theguardian.com/world/2016/may/11/the-cultural-revolution-50-years-on-all-you-need-to-know-about-chinas-political-convulsion. Accessed 10 February 2018.

[1] Oakley, Barbara. *Evil Genes: Why Rome Fell, Hitler Rose, Enron Failed, and My Sister Stole My Mother's Boyfriend.* 2007.

[1] "Red Guards." *Encyclopædia Britannica.* https://www.britannica.com/topic/Red-Guards. Accessed 10 February 2018.

[1] Ramzy, Austin. "China's Cultural Revolution, Explained". *The New York Times.* May 2016. https://www.nytimes.com/2016/05/15/world/asia/china-cultural-revolution-explainer.html?module=Slide&region=SlideShowTopBar&version=SlideCard-8&action=Click&contentCollection=Asia%20Pacific&slideshowTitle=Mao%E2%80%99s%20Cultural%20Revolution&currentSlide=8&entrySlide=1&pgtype=imageslideshow. Accessed 10 February 2018.

[1] Mao, Yu Run. "Music under Mao, Its Background and Aftermath". *Asian Music.* 1991.

[1] "Consequences of the Cultural Revolution." *Encyclopædia Britannica.* https://www.britannica.com/place/China/Consequences-of-the-Cultural-Revolution#ref71860. Accessed 10 February 2018.

[1] "Jiang Qing." *Encyclopædia Britannica.* https://www.britannica.com/biography/Jiang-Qing. Accessed 10 February 2018.

[1] Phillips, Tom. "The Cultural Revolution: All You Need to Know about China's Political Convulsion." *The Guardian.* May 2016. https://www.theguardian.com/world/2016/may/11/the-cultural-revolution-50-years-on-all-you-need-to-know-about-chinas-political-convulsion. Accessed 10 February 2018.

[1] Ibid.

[1] Koerner, Brendan. "What's a Maoist, Anyway?" *Slate.* February 2004. http://www.slate.com/articles/news_and_politics/explainer/2004/02/whats_a_maoist_anyway.html. Accessed 10 February 2018.

[1] Bernstein, Richard. "The Tyrant Mao, as Told by His Doctor". October 1994. *The New York Times.*

http://www.nytimes.com/1994/10/02/world/the-tyrant-mao-as-told-by-his-doctor.html?pagewanted=all. Accessed 10 February 2018.

[1] Phillips, Tom. "In China Women 'Hold Up Half the Sky' but Can't Touch the Political Glass Ceiling." *The Guardian.* Oct 2017. https://www.theguardian.com/world/2017/oct/14/in-china-women-hold-up-half-the-sky-but-cant-touch-the-political-glass-ceiling. Accessed 10 February 2018.

[1] Gao, Helen. "How Did Women Fare in China's Communist Revolution?" *The New York Times.* Sep 2017. https://www.nytimes.com/2017/09/25/opinion/women-china-communist-revolution.html?smid=tw-nytopinion&smtyp=cur&mtrref=www.theguardian.com&assetType=opinion. Accessed 10 February 2018.

[1] Bo, Zhiyue. "Mao Zedong: Savior or Demon?". *The Diplomat.* December 2015. https://thediplomat.com/2015/12/mao-zedong-savior-or-demon/. Accessed 10 February 2018.

Bibliography for Mao Zedong

1964: The Little Red Book, Justin G. Schiller, October 30, 2014, The New Antiquarian, www.abaa.org/blog/

53a. McCarthyism, U.S. History, 2019, www.ushistory.org/

A Brief Overview of China's Cultural Revolution, The Editor of Encyclopedia Britannica, 2019, Encyclopedia Britannica, https://www.britannica.com/story/chinas-cultural-revolution

China Turned Upside Down: Life During Mao's Bloody, Chaotic Cultural Revolution, Weijian Shan, January 26, 2019, Foreign Affairs, https://www.foreignaffairs.com/articles/china/2019-01-26/china-turned-upside-down

China's Cultural Revolution in Memories: The CR/10 Project, University of Pittsburgh, 2015, https://digital.library.pitt.edu/collection/chinas-cultural-revolution-memories-the-CR10-project

China's Cultural Revolution, Stanford University, 2019, https://sheg.stanford.edu/history-lessons/chinas-cultural-revolution

China's Red Guards, Kallie Szczepanski, October 22, 2019, Thought Co., www.thoughtco.com/

Chinese History: First Five-Year Plan (1953-1957), Lauren Mack, March 11, 2018, ThoughtCo, www.thoughtco.com/

Chinese Red Guards Apologize, Reopening a Dark Chapter, Anthony Kuhn, February 4, 2014, npr, www.npr.org/

Chronology of Mass Killings during the Chinese Cultural Revolution (1966-1976), Yongyi Song, August 25, 2011, SciencesPro, www.sciencespo.fr/

Communist China, Lumen, 2019, lumencandela, https://courses.lumenlearning.com/boundless-worldhistory/chapter/communist-china/

Communist Leaders and Their Policies, Australian Government, 2018, Years of Anzac, anzacportal.dva.gov.au/history/

Cultural Revolution, History.com Editors, Jun 6, 2019, History, https://www.history.com/topics/china/cultural-revolution

Debating the Cultural Revolution in China, Mao's Last Revolution, Roderick MacFarquhar, Michael Schoenhals, Dr Julia Lovella, 2006, November 2, 2019, https://reviews.history.ac.uk/review/1179

Deng Xiaoping, chineseposters.net, October 13, 2019, chineseposters.net/themes/dengxiaoping.php

Exploring Chinese History, Richard R. Wertz, 2017, Exploring Chinese History, www.ibiblio.org/chinesehistory/

Great Leap Forward (1958-1961), October 13, 2019, chineseposters.net, chineseposters.net/themes/great-leap-forward.php

How Staling Elevated the Chinese Communist Party to Power in Xinjiang in 1949, Charles Kraus, May 11, 2018, Wilson Center, www.wilsoncenter.org

How the Soviet Union and China almost Started World War III, Robert Farley, February 9, 2016, The National Interest, nationalinterest.org/

Khrushchev in Water Wings: On Mao, Humiliation and the Sino-Soviet Split, Mike Dash, May 4, 2012, Smithsonian, www.smithsonianmag.com/

Lin Biao, October 13, 2019, chineseposters.net, chineseposters.net/themes/linbiao.php

Liu Shaoqi, chineseposters.net, October 13, 2019, chineseposters.net/themes/liushaoqi.php

Ma Zedong's China Unrecognizable 40 Years on from His Death, Jamil Anderlini, September 9, 2016, Financial Times, www.ft.com/

Mao Tse-tung (1893 * 1976) – His Habits and His Health, Samj Forum, 2019, Health and Medical Publishing Group, www.scielo.org.za/

Mao Zedong (1893-1976), ExEAS, 2019, www.columbia.edu/cu/weai/exeas/

Mao Zedong: Chinese Leader, Stuart Reynolds Schram, October 11, 2019, Encyclopedia Britannica, www.britannica.com

May Fourth Movement (1919), June 24, 2017, Chow Tse-Tung, Rana Mitter, chineseposters.net, chineseposters.net/themes/may-fourth-movement.php

Nikita Khrushchev: Premier of Soviet Union, Frank B. Gibney, 2019, Encyclopedia Britannica, www.britannica.com/

Nixon's Great Decision on China, 40 Years Later, David Ignatius, February 10, 2012, The Washington Post, www.washingtonpost.com/

Overview of the Chinese Cultural Revolution, Kallie Szczepanski, August 9, 2019, Thought Co, https://www.thoughtco.com/what-was-the-cultural-revolution-195607

Readjustment and Reaction, 1961-1965, Encyclopedia Britannica, 2019, www.britannica.com/

Rise and Fall of Lin Biao (1969-71), Kenneth G. Lieberthal, 2019, Encyclopedia Britannica, www.britannica.com/

Sino-Soviet Border Clashes, John Pike, 2019, Globalsecurity, www.globalsecurity.org/

The Cultural Revolution and Its Legacies in International Perspective, The China Quarterly, Julia Lovell, September 2016, https://www.cambridge.org/core/journals/china-quarterly/article/cultural-revolution-and-its-legacies-in-international-perspective/AF89666FAABFC3AB33B5AB5C32FE41E1/core-reader

The Cultural Revolution: All You Need to Know about China's Political Convulsion, Tom Phillips, May 10, 2016, The Guardian, https://www.theguardian.com/world/2016/may/11/the-cultural-revolution-50-years-on-all-you-need-to-know-about-chinas-political-convulsion

The Great leap Forward, Kallie Szcepanski, September 3, 2019, ThoughtCo., www.thoughtco.com/

The Great Proletarian Cultural Revolution in China, 1966 – 1976, Thayer Walkins, San José State University, 2019, http://www.sjsu.edu/faculty/watkins/cultrev.htm

The Great Tangshan Earthquake of 1976, Kallie Szczepanski, January 30, 2019, ThoughtCo., www.thoughtco.com/

The Rise of Mao Zedong, Glenn Kucha, Jennifer Llewellyn, November 15, 2019, alpha history, alphahistory.com/chineserevolution/rise-of-mao-zedong/

The Sino-Soviet Border War: Why the USSR nearly Nuked China, Tom Garner, August 24, 2016, History of War, www.historyanswers.co.uk/

Walder, Andrew G. 2009, *Fractured Rebellions: The Beijing Red Guard Movement*, Cambridge: Harvard University Press.

What Was the Gang of Four in China?, Kallie Szczepanski, July 23, 2019, ThoughtCo., www.thoughtco.com/

Why the Peninsula Is Split into North Korea and South Korea, Kallie Szcepanski, July 18, 2019, ThoughtCo., www.thoughtco.com/

---

[i] Buruma, Ian. "Cult of the Chairman." March 2001. *The Guardian.* https://www.theguardian.com/world/2001/mar/07/china.features11. Accessed 10 February 2018.

ii "Deng Xiaoping." *Encyclopædia Britannica.* hhttps://www.britannica.com/biography/Deng-Xiaoping. Accessed 10 February 2018.

iii Oakley, Barbara. *Evil Genes: Why Rome Fell, Hitler Rose, Enron Failed, and My Sister Stole My Mother's Boyfriend.* 2007.

iv Kristof, Nicholas D. "Legacy of Mao Called 'Great Disaster." *The New York Times.* February 1989. http://www.nytimes.com/1989/02/07/world/legacy-of-mao-called-great-disaster.html. Accessed 10 February 2018.

v Pantsov, Alexander and Levine, Steven I. *Mao: The Real Story.* 2012.

vi Ibid.

vii Chang, Jung and Halliday, Jon. *Mao: The Unknown Story.* 2005.

viii Snow, Edgar. *Red Star over China.* 1937.

ix Pantsov, Alexander and Levine, Steven I. *Mao: The Real Story.* 2012.

x Ibid.

xi Ibid.

xii "Changsha." *Encyclopædia Britannica.* https://www.britannica.com/place/Changsha. Accessed 10 February 2018.

xiii "Sun Yat-sen." *Encyclopædia Britannica.* https://www.britannica.com/biography/Sun-Yat-sen. Accessed 10 February 2018.

xiv Pantsov, Alexander and Levine, Steven I. *Mao: The Real Story.* 2012.

xv Snow, Edgar. *Red Star over China.* 1937.

xvi Pantsov, Alexander and Levine, Steven I. *Mao: The Real Story.* 2012.

xvii Ibid.

[xviii] Schram, Stuart Reynolds. *Mao's Road to Power vol. 1: Pre-Marxist Period, 1912-20.* 1992.

[xix] Pantsov, Alexander and Levine, Steven I. *Mao: The Real Story.* 2012.

[xx] Ibid.

[xxi] "May Fourth Movement." *Encyclopædia Britannica.* https://www.britannica.com/event/May-Fourth-Movement. Accessed 10 February 2018

[xxii] Schram, Stuart Reynolds. *Mao's Road to Power vol. 1: Pre-Marxist Period, 1912-20.* 1992.

[xxiii] "Russian Revolution of 1917." *Encyclopædia Britannica.* https://www.britannica.com/event/Russian-Revolution-of-1917. Accessed 10 February 2018.

[xxiv] Chang, Jung and Halliday, Jon. *Mao: The Unknown Story.* 2005.

[xxv] Pantsov, Alexander and Levine, Steven I. *Mao: The Real Story.* 2012.

[xxvi] Schram, Stuart Reynolds. *Mao's Road to Power vol. 1: Pre-Marxist Period, 1912-20.* 1992.

[xxvii] "Chinese Communist Party." *Encyclopædia Britannica.* https://www.britannica.com/topic/Chinese-Communist-Party. Accessed 10 February 2018.

[xxviii] Ch'en, Kung-po. *The Communist Movement in China: An Essay Written in 1924.* 1966.

[xxix] "Nationalist Party." *Encyclopædia Britannica.* https://www.britannica.com/topic/Nationalist-Party-Chinese-political-party. Accessed 10 February 2018.

[xxx] Pantsov, Alexander and Levine, Steven I. *Mao: The Real Story.* 2012.

[xxxi] Snow, Edgar. *Red Star over China.* 1937.

[xxxii] Pantsov, Alexander and Levine, Steven I. *Mao: The Real Story.* 2012.

[xxxiii] "Three Principles of the People." *Encyclopædia Britannica.* https://www.britannica.com/event/Three-Principles-of-the-People. Accessed 10 February 2018.

[xxxiv] Schram, Stuart Reynolds. *Mao's Road to Power vol. 2: National Revolution and Social Revolution, December 1920-June 1927.* 1992.

[xxxv] Pantsov, Alexander and Levine, Steven I. *Mao: The Real Story.* 2012.

[xxxvi] "Chiang Kai-shek". *Encyclopædia Britannica.* https://www.britannica.com/biography/Chiang-Kai-shek. Accessed 10 February 2018.

[xxxvii] Ibid.

[xxxviii] "Northern Expedition". *Encyclopædia Britannica.* https://www.britannica.com/event/Northern-Expedition. Accessed 10 February 2018.

[xxxix] Mao, Zedong. *Selected Works of Mao Tse-Tung: Volume 1.* 1965.

[xl] "People's Liberation Army". *Encyclopædia Britannica.* https://www.britannica.com/topic/Peoples-Liberation-Army-Chinese-army. Accessed 10 February 2018.

[xli] Chang, Jung and Halliday, Jon. *Mao: The Unknown Story.* 2005.

[xlii] "Jiangxi Soviet". *Encyclopædia Britannica.* https://www.britannica.com/topic/Jiangxi-Soviet. Accessed 10 February 2018.

[xliii] Mao, Zedong. "Respectfully Quoted: A Dictionary of Quotations." *Bartleby.* http://www.bartleby.com/73/1933.html. Accessed 10 February 2018.

[xliv] "Mukden Incident". *Encyclopædia Britannica.* https://www.britannica.com/event/Mukden-Incident. Accessed 10 February 2018.

[xlv] "Long March". *Encyclopædia Britannica.* https://www.britannica.com/event/Long-March. Accessed 10 February 2018.

[xlvi] Ibid.

[xlvii] Lau, Mimi. "The Long March: What it was and why it Matters to China's Xi Jinping." *South China Morning Post.* October 2016. http://www.scmp.com/news/china/policies-politics/article/2039033/long-march-what-it-was-and-why-it-matters. Accessed 10 February 2018.

[xlviii] "Establishment of the People's Republic". *Encyclopædia Britannica.* https://www.britannica.com/place/China/Establishment-of-the-Peoples-Republic. Accessed 10 February 2018.

[xlix] "Reconstruction and Consolidation, 1949–52". *Encyclopædia Britannica.* https://www.britannica.com/place/China/Reconstruction-and-consolidation-1949-52. Accessed 10 February 2018.

[l] "Korean War." *Encyclopædia Britannica.* https://www.britannica.com/event/Korean-War. Accessed 10 February 2018.

[li] "First Five-Year Plan." *Encyclopædia Britannica.* https://www.britannica.com/topic/First-Five-Year-Plan-Chinese-economics. Accessed 10 February 2018.

[lii] "Hundred Flowers Campaign." *Encyclopædia Britannica.* https://www.britannica.com/event/Hundred-Flowers-Campaign. Accessed 10 February 2018.

[liii] "Commune." *Encyclopædia Britannica.* https://www.britannica.com/topic/commune-Chinese-agriculture. Accessed 10 February 2018.

[liv] "Great Leap Forward." *Encyclopædia Britannica.* https://www.britannica.com/event/Great-Leap-Forward. Accessed 10 February 2018.

[lv] Dikötter, Frank. "Mao's Great Leap to Famine." *The New York Times.* December 2010. http://www.nytimes.com/2010/12/16/opinion/16iht-eddikotter16.html?mtrref=undefined&gwh=B68D2BA84DBA7794C6E54CBC9EB5EC30&gwt=pay&assetType=opinion. Accessed 10 February 2018.

[lvi] Ibid.

[lvii] "Hai Rui Dismissed From Office." *Encyclopædia Britannica.* https://www.britannica.com/topic/Gang-of-Four#ref213744. Accessed 10 February 2018.

[lviii] "Peng Dehuai." *Encyclopædia Britannica.* https://www.britannica.com/biography/Peng-Dehuai. Accessed 10 February 2018.

[lix] "Gang of Four." *Encyclopædia Britannica.* https://www.britannica.com/topic/Hai-Rui-Dismissed-From-Office. Accessed 10 February 2018.

[lx] "Cultural Revolution." *Encyclopædia Britannica.* https://www.britannica.com/event/Cultural-Revolution. Accessed 10 February 2018.

[lxi] "Liu Shaoqi." *Encyclopædia Britannica.* https://www.britannica.com/biography/Liu-Shaoqi. Accessed 10 February 2018.

[lxii] Phillips, Tom. "The Cultural Revolution: All You Need to Know about China's Political Convulsion." *The Guardian.* May 2016. https://www.theguardian.com/world/2016/may/11/the-cultural-revolution-50-years-on-all-you-need-to-know-about-chinas-political-convulsion. Accessed 10 February 2018.

[lxiii] Oakley, Barbara. *Evil Genes: Why Rome Fell, Hitler Rose, Enron Failed, and My Sister Stole My Mother's Boyfriend.* 2007.

[lxiv] "Red Guards." *Encyclopædia Britannica.* https://www.britannica.com/topic/Red-Guards. Accessed 10 February 2018.

[lxv] Ramzy, Austin. "China's Cultural Revolution, Explained". *The New York Times.* May 2016. https://www.nytimes.com/2016/05/15/world/asia/china-cultural-revolution-explainer.html?module=Slide&region=SlideShowTopBar&version=SlideCard-8&action=Click&contentCollection=Asia%20Pacific&slideshowTitle=Mao%E2%80%99s%20Cultural%20Revolution&currentSlide=8&entrySlide=1&pgtype=imageslideshow. Accessed 10 February 2018.

[lxvi] Mao, Yu Run. "Music under Mao, Its Background and Aftermath". *Asian Music.* 1991.

[lxvii] "Consequences of the Cultural Revolution." *Encyclopædia Britannica.* https://www.britannica.com/place/China/Consequences-of-the-Cultural-Revolution#ref71860. Accessed 10 February 2018.

[lxviii] "Jiang Qing." *Encyclopædia Britannica.* https://www.britannica.com/biography/Jiang-Qing. Accessed 10 February 2018.

[lxix] Phillips, Tom. "The Cultural Revolution: All You Need to Know about China's Political Convulsion." *The Guardian.* May 2016. https://www.theguardian.com/world/2016/may/11/the-cultural-revolution-50-years-on-all-you-need-to-know-about-chinas-political-convulsion. Accessed 10 February 2018.

[lxx] Ibid.

[lxxi] Koerner, Brendan. "What's a Maoist, Anyway?" *Slate.* February 2004. http://www.slate.com/articles/news_and_politics/explainer/2004/02/whats_a_maoist_anyway.html. Accessed 10 February 2018.

[lxxii] Bernstein, Richard. "The Tyrant Mao, as Told by His Doctor". October 1994. *The New York Times.* http://www.nytimes.com/1994/10/02/world/the-tyrant-mao-as-told-by-his-doctor.html?pagewanted=all. Accessed 10 February 2018.

[lxxiii] Phillips, Tom. "In China Women 'Hold Up Half the Sky' but Can't Touch the Political Glass Ceiling." *The Guardian.* Oct 2017. https://www.theguardian.com/world/2017/oct/14/in-china-women-hold-up-half-the-sky-but-cant-touch-the-political-glass-ceiling. Accessed 10 February 2018.

[lxxiv] Gao, Helen. "How Did Women Fare in China's Communist Revolution?" *The New York Times.* Sep 2017. https://www.nytimes.com/2017/09/25/opinion/women-china-communist-revolution.html?smid=tw-nytopinion&smtyp=cur&mtrref=www.theguardian.com&assetType=opinion. Accessed 10 February 2018.

[lxxv] Bo, Zhiyue. "Mao Zedong: Savior or Demon?". *The Diplomat*. December 2015. https://thediplomat.com/2015/12/mao-zedong-savior-or-demon/. Accessed 10 February 2018.